R.A. RANNEY
234 Shaughnessy Blvd.
North York, Ontario M2J 1K8
(416) 494 3539

UNDERGROUND NATION

UNDERGROUND NATION

THE SECRET ECONOMY AND THE FUTURE OF CANADA

DIANE FRANCIS

KEY PORTER BOOKS

Canadian Cataloguing in Publication Data

Francis, Diane
   Underground nation : the secret economy
   and the future of Canada

ISBN 1-55013-612-7

1. Commercial crimes — Canada. 2. Informal sector (Economics) —
Canada. 3. Canada — Economic conditions — 1991– .* I. Title.

HC115.F73 1994   330.971'0647   C94-931630-X

Key Porter Books Limited
70 The Esplanade
Toronto, Ontario
Canada M5E 1R2

Typesetting: MacTrix dtp

Printed and bound in Canada

94 95 96 97 98 99 6 5 4 3 2

CONTENTS

Canadians are not leaving their country.
Their country has left them.
— Vancouver entrepreneur Jimmy Pattison

INTRODUCTION

CANADA AS WE KNOW IT SIMPLY WILL NOT SURVIVE. Already the country is slipping away before our very eyes. Discontent, cheating, and underground economic activity have become widespread in response to the high taxes resulting from two decades' worth of poor governance. Our accumulated debt has dramatically devalued our currency since 1992, and we are moving toward a crisis. While it is appropriate that attention be focused on the debt, the fact is that it is not the root cause of Canada's problem. Debt is only the reflection of flaws in the nation-state. And Canadians instinctively know this. It is surely significant that, in the October 1993 federal election, one in three Canadians voted for a new Canada by casting a ballot for the untested, unknown Reform Party or the explicitly separatist Bloc Québécois.

What is especially frustrating when examining Canada's problems is that they are easily fixed. If politicians just

1

adopted one-quarter of the solutions I recommend later in this book, the country would right itself. Canada remains one of the world's luckiest nations, unburdened with a huge underclass, monstrous crime rate, insecure borders, a deluge of illegal aliens, warlike neighbours, or corruption. Canada's only problem is that its leaders have been second-rate, borrowing too much money for two decades then spending it unwisely to feather their own political nests.

We have suffered from mediocre, arrogant government for more than twenty years, because Canada's democracy has never broken out of its colonial traditions. Majority governments rule like dictatorships, fostering a corrupt and inefficient system that is not sufficiently accountable to the electorate. The ultimate evidence of their arrogance is the fact that these governments have routinely overspent their budgets since the early 1970s, confident that they can simply tax Canadians as much as they need to. Now Canada's debt burden threatens the sovereignty of the country itself.

Governments spend more of our hard-earned money on interest payments than on our health care system. Within five years, these interest payments could be bigger than health and education expenditures combined. By the turn of the century, Canadians will be committed to paying off lenders and getting few, if any, government services in return. This is a formula for disaster.

During the 1980s, governments increased taxes from 31 per cent of the economy, or gross domestic product (GDP), to 39 per cent — second only to the tax hikes imposed in a financially troubled Italy. These increases were necessary because the national debt climbed 500 per cent between 1981 and 1994. In the four years of Liberal rule which ended on March 31, 1985, the country's debts nearly tripled, to

$202.4 billion. In their nine years of stewardship, Brian Mulroney and his Tories doubled the debt they inherited. By the time of the federal election in October 1993, Canada's debts topped $470 billion. That was bad enough, but during this same period the provinces ran amok. The combined provincial debt in 1982 was a mere $11.2 billion. By 1994, it had soared to $155 billion, an increase of more than 1,300 per cent. The provinces were left to their own foolish devices by both Liberals and Tories in Ottawa; both parties were spending too much time currying the provinces' favour for constitutional reasons to discipline them.

The taxes Canadians pay have soared. In fiscal year 1981–82, 11 million Canadian workers paid a per-capita average of $2,293 in federal taxes and another $1,499 in provincial income taxes. By 1992–93, some 12.3 million Canadians were employed, but each was handing over an average of $5,355 in federal income tax, and $3,221 in provincial tax, per year. So taxes have nearly tripled in eleven years, from $3,792 per person to $8,576, even though taxpayers are not getting more for their money.

So there you have it: in a ten-year period, the economy went up by nearly 200 per cent; taxes by 300 per cent; federal debts by 500 per cent; and provincial debts by an unbelievable 1,300 per cent. Worse yet, some 40 per cent of all debts are owed to foreigners. By 1994, Canadians were sending $100 million per day out of the country in the form of interest payments to foreign lenders in New York, Frankfurt, or Tokyo. This money represents $1 out of every $20 generated by the entire economy, and is a permanent loss of wealth on a scale that no country can sustain. That money neither returns nor is spent in Canada to create jobs or generate more taxes. Clearly, spending is totally out of control in

Canada, but our politicians are doing nothing about it.

Their inaction is attributable to two causes. First, there is the misguided hope that the economy will grow enough to reduce the impact of debts. Second, there is the fact that the nations of the world compete in a form of reverse beauty contest. By this, I mean that, as far as lenders are concerned, there are no "beauties" in the world. Some countries are just less ugly than others. And Canada, despite debts, is considerably less ugly than Argentina, Mexico, Slovakia, or South Korea. These other countries have enormous potential military, border, religious, or ideological problems. Canada enjoys protection because of its proximity to the United States, has valuable free-trade arrangements in North America, and has demonstrated so far that it can tax Canadians to meet its debt obligations.

Winning the world's reverse beauty contest may ultimately prove to be a curse, as increasing numbers of Canadians avoid or evade taxes, hide their assets offshore, or leave the country. The October 1993 federal election underscored the seriousness of the discontent. Two mainstream political parties — the Progressive Conservatives and New Democrats — were obliterated. Millions of voters gave their support instead to the two new upstart populist parties, the Reform Party and Bloc Québécois. The two new parties garnered a combined popular vote of 33 per cent. The successful Liberals were able to form a majority government after winning only 41 per cent of the vote because of the massive amount of vote-splitting between the Reform Party and Conservatives in English Canada. Liberal support is soft. Some 8.25 per cent of their 41 per cent popular vote was from Quebec, where frightened federalists voted Liberal to prevent the election of separatists.

One in three voters in Canada was angry enough to cast a ballot for a party whose candidates were largely unknown and whose goals were, in essence, to destroy Canada as we know it. The year before, 53 per cent of Canadians had rejected the Charlottetown Accord proposals and, by so doing, rejected the country's entire political leadership. Both events revealed the extent to which Canada's governments are out of step with a public which grows angrier and more rebellious as each year passes. Instead of coming to grips with the real problems they face, our politicians remain preoccupied with getting re-elected, pandering to Quebec, or placating certain favoured special-interest groups, particularly the unions. In their rush to please a few, they alienate the many by limiting freedom of speech, linguistic rights, and individual liberties. Pandering to minorities has led to the deification of multiculturalism, which divides our society.

Today a significant percentage of the population perceives the taxation burden as onerous and unfair. Poor government stewardship has forced many corporations and entrepreneurs to leave the country or move profit centres offshore. The inevitable consequence will be an erosion of the tax base and ever-growing deficits.

Contributing to the disillusionment felt by many Canadians is the scandalous incompetence of governments which indiscriminately and carelessly hand out health and welfare benefits. Politicians consistently and irrationally deny the extent of fraud that exists in the system, with severely damaging effects on the economy. Unfortunately, abuse tends to lead to further abuse as embittered Canadians take the view that since everybody else is ripping off the system, they might as well rip it off too.

Canadians are demanding change, but the chances of their getting it are not good. The Liberal version of federalism, like the Tory version that preceded it, promises to do nothing but cater to Quebec for as long as its mandate runs. By the late 1990s, chances are the country's debts will have doubled and, indeed, the country may have ceased to exist.

Canada is not the only nation-state whose existence is threatened. All nation-states will experience massive change in the next century because the reasons for their existence — economic organization and defence — are disappearing. Global free trade has erased the need to be part of a captive market, and the end of the Cold War has transferred military burdens to the United Nations and away from individual countries.

This is the paradox of the post–Cold War world: globalization erodes the importance and power of the traditional nation-state, while at the same time people seek smaller, more responsive government units in the face of internationalization. As they do so, the lower levels of government also eat away at the nation-state as they assume social and cultural responsibilities on a more homogeneous basis. In Canada's case, the federal government has, over the decades, handed over enormous power to the provinces, and now also to the North American Free Trade Agreement (NAFTA) as well as the General Agreement on Tariffs and Trade (GATT). Logically, this means Ottawa should massively downsize. Its role should be to manage the overall economy and to act as a coordinating body among provinces and between Canadians and the rest of the world. Instead, Ottawa's politicians and bureaucrats have been resisting worldwide trends and jealously guarding their power. What may kill this country is not devolution of more power to Quebec and the other provinces, but the notion that an unpopular, unamendable constitution and control of the tax purse strings can impose a unitary state on Canadians.

Canada is drowning in debt, but, for the time being, life

goes on as usual for most Canadians. There is high unemployment, but for those of us who have jobs, the living is easy. Canadians enjoy the world's second-highest standard of living. We dine out, own our own homes, have good-paying jobs, take holidays, own cottages, drive more than one car, and fool around with boats and a range of electronic gadgets.

But Canada's deficit-dependent economy is artificially inflated by 10 per cent as a result of overspending by governments based on foreign borrowing. We do not feel the full negative effects of debt-servicing costs because governments keep borrowing the money to make their interest payments on debts. This simply cannot continue. Weaning ourselves from an indebted lifestyle will be painful. Living standards for the lower and middle classes will plummet. University tuition will quadruple. Health care charges will be imposed. The unemployed will have to live on considerably less, or on their families' charity. Services of all kinds will disappear.

Canadians will survive, but the country will be transformed. There are a number of solutions I've outlined which could turn the country around in time. Canada, like IBM and other companies that have reinvented themselves, will not restructure until it is forced to. Tragically, it may take an exchange-rate crisis or secession by Quebec to bring about the needed reforms. The danger is that these crises may also bring about chaos or forced amalgamation with the United States.

THE FLIGHT
OF CAPITAL

OTTAWA SIMPLY DOES NOT GET IT. WHEN FACED WITH complaints about high taxes, government officials have been known to point out that Canadian taxes are not excessive compared with those of other industrialized nations. After all, they say, Canada's taxes in 1993 reached 39.4 per cent of its GDP, while Sweden's hit 51.7 per cent and the Netherlands' 47.2 per cent. But the only comparison that matters is with the United States, where taxes are equivalent to only 29.6 per cent of GDP. Swedish governments have been able to impose such high taxes because their citizens are tax captives who cannot easily emigrate or take their capital out of the country. Canadians, however, have options, and they are taking advantage of them by evading, avoiding, hiding assets, or leaving.

"Tax resentment is sizeable in Canada, and resentment isn't an absolute thing. It's all relative, and Canadians compare their taxes to American levels," pointed out David Perry, an

8

analyst with the Canadian Tax Foundation, a non-profit think-tank in Toronto which studies taxes. "We never had a situation like this and we're about at the limit compared to the United States. Canadian taxpayers also look at whether their dollars are getting them services commensurate with what they are paying or would pay elsewhere. The fact is that here we are providing more money to governments, getting less, and the deficit isn't falling. The resentment is very high."

Varity Corporation's CEO, financial expert, and world corporate traveller Victor Rice cited high taxes as one of the reasons why Varity, formerly Canadian transnational Massey-Ferguson, moved its head office in 1991 to Buffalo, New York, from Toronto. He said tax resistance is a worldwide phenomenon. "When marginal tax rates hit 50 per cent, something happens in every country. It's at that point that a person — anyone from anywhere — begins to cheat. That seems to be the psychological threshold, and Canada's beyond that."

Canadian leaders must understand that the world's economies are rapidly integrating, and money can be moved electronically in nanoseconds. They must also realize that Canadians enjoy more access to passports and places to live than do virtually any other nation's citizens. This means Canada's governments, companies, and individuals must behave in completely different ways. They are service-giving organizations. If a business overcharges for its services, its customers go elsewhere or keep their money to themselves. The business loses money and eventually folds. The same thing can happen to nations.

Tax burdens were to blame, in part, for the fall of the Roman Empire because Romans balked at paying the huge taxes needed to support a large army and so left themselves vulnerable to invasion. Lutherans and Jansonists successfully attacked, and eventually unravelled, the hegemony of the medieval Roman Catholic Church of Europe by attacking the church's extravagances and the sale of "indulgences" (pieces of paper forgiving sins). More recently, Britain lost its thirteen colonies in America when a handful of taxpayers threw tea into Boston harbour.

Canada's governments are also losing the consent of the taxed. Some people understand this. The first glimmer of hope for those who want reform of the tax system was seen in early 1994 when Quebec forced Ottawa to reduce taxes on tobacco and charge the same as Americans were charging in order to stop massive smuggling and open defiance of the law. A number of provincial governments followed grudgingly. Most do not yet understand that they must reduce any taxes that exceed those charged in the United States. Canadian taxpayers, not just Canadian smokers, will avoid or evade taxes if they possibly can.

THE UNDERGROUND

More and more Canadians are starting to realize that other Canadians are cheating, bending the rules, or hiding money offshore. Attitudes in Canada have shifted dangerously toward a them-versus-us stance which feeds on itself, guaranteeing even more cheating. Polls show that it has become socially acceptable, for example, to half of Canadians to evade the hated Goods and Services Tax (GST) by paying cash under the table.

No one knows exactly how big the underground economy has become. David Perry guesses that it is between 8.5 and 15 per cent of the GDP, and growing. At 15 per cent, that would amount to $10,000 per family per year, the equivalent of the GDP of Alberta and British Columbia combined. "But the bigger change is that the other taxpayers' attitudes have changed when they are shopping or filling in their tax return. They say, 'If others are tax evading, so will I,'" said Perry.

That change of attitude is a direct response to the tax hikes Canadians have been subjected to since 1981. That year the average Canadian worker paid $3,792 in taxes. By 1991–92, the average was $8,576. As a proportion of the GDP, Canada's personal income taxes at 15.2 per cent are fifth-highest among the two dozen wealthy members of the Organization for Economic Cooperation and Development (OECD), where the average is 11.7 per cent. Taxes have nearly tripled in Canada since 1981, but incomes certainly have not, nor are taxpayers getting more for their money.

Canadians who work for others can cheat only by paying cash for goods and services. The GST focused the minds of Canadians on their tax problems and probably destroyed the Tory party federally. But it is interesting to note that Canadians had been paying an even higher "GST" for twenty years in the form of a hidden manufacturers' sales tax. When that tax was made visible, all hell broke loose.

"The GST is not a new tax but went from invisible to visible. We're complaining about a tax load some Europeans lived with for a long time. But the newness, visibility, and comparison to the U.S. makes the GST so objectionable," said David Perry.

Canada's employed bear the brunt of taxes, but the shift toward self-employment — made by 7.3 per cent of the workforce since the mid-1980s — has facilitated cheating. The self-employed pay considerably lower taxes, given the same income, because they can write off living expenses and frills that employees cannot write off. They also pay only 22 per cent corporate income taxes on earnings up to $200,000 in most provinces. Employed individuals at that level are in the 56 per cent range.

The self-employed can take advantage of other dodges, and they are often assisted in perpetrating their minor frauds. They can, and often do, ask cab drivers for blank receipts. Restaurants routinely give business patrons their credit card receipt plus a blank so they can easily make a second claim and pump up expenses artificially. Retailers routinely make out invoices to a company name for carpeting, house paint, tools, or car parts, even though the items are acquired for personal use. Such tax-evasion tricks are rarely detected because it is impossible for Revenue Canada to investigate all cash receipts submitted by Canada's 2.5 million businesses. The result of the favourable treatment enjoyed by the self-employed, plus aggressive write-offs by many, is that Canada collected the equivalent of only 1.6 per cent of GDP from its self-employed, compared with an OECD average of 5.1 per cent.

Meanwhile, Canada's 12.3 million employed get even any way they can. As tourists abroad, many routinely smuggle goods into the country. It's relatively easy to get away with smuggling by choosing a busy point of entry and a busy day — like a holiday weekend — when border guards can stop and inspect cars on only an occasional, random basis. Others cheerfully declare what they're bringing into the country, but lie about the number of trips abroad they've taken, in order to exceed the limit on annual imports. This, too, is easy because the customs department cross-references customs declarations by name and date of birth. To beat the system, travellers need only alter their date of birth by a single digit.

Similarly, people crossing borders with contraband in the

trunks of their cars or under their clothing are also adept at getting through unnoticed, choosing the busiest times of day when border guards are prevented by traffic jams from being systematic in their inspections.

The perception that cheating is rampant is widespread. A 1994 poll by KPMG Peat Marwick Thorne showed a dangerous shift in attitudes toward paying taxes. Some 19 per cent of Canadians who were polled said they would hide income if they could get away with it; 26 per cent said they would buy smuggled cigarettes or booze; 32 per cent said they would smuggle goods into the country without declaring their value; and 49 per cent said they would pay cash to avoid the GST and provincial sales taxes.

Some 56 per cent polled said the tax system was unfair to average Canadians, and 42 per cent said they do not get good value for their tax dollars. KPMG noted as "alarming" the attitudes toward cheating. Only 22 per cent said they were model citizens who paid all their taxes; 28 per cent said they were honest but resentful; 34 per cent said they were upset and envious of those who could cheat; and 16 per cent were "tax anarchists" who avoided taxes whenever possible. "Canadians overwhelmingly feel their tax money is wasted. There is also a significant element of social acceptability to evasion," the report's authors concluded.

The level of acceptance is sometimes amusing. In a television interview in 1993, I was asked about tobacco smuggling and the underground economy. I called for tax and price parity as the only means of solving the problem. Another interviewee called for Draconian action by governments, crackdowns at the border, and spot audits to catch cheating tradesmen. But as the two of us left the studio, he pulled out a pack of cigarettes and offered me one. They were obviously American cigarettes, lacking the health warning required in Canada, which meant that they were almost certainly contraband. The point is that he did not seem to be aware of his own hypocrisy. Canadians often do not consider the consequences of their behaviour. Then again, neither do their governments.

The result is a huge underground economy. The federal government consistently pooh-poohs the claims made by the Canadian Tax Foundation and others about the scale on which the underground economy now operates. A Statistics Canada report in 1994 suggested that the underground economy amounted to no more than 2.7 per cent of GDP, or $10 billion. According to Statistics Canada, illegal economic activity on a larger scale would be reflected in higher employment figures, increased car sales, and booming restaurant business. This interpretation of the facts is naïve. It ignores, for example, the sum of Canadian-earned cash that is spent flamboyantly outside of Canada. It ignores the fact that retailers in Christmas 1992 and 1993 were taken aback by the sudden and unaccounted-for jump in sales. And it ignores the otherwise baffling fact that by 1993 there were $100 billion more banknotes in circulation than existed before the GST.

The anecdotal evidence is overwhelming that the black market is vast. Everyone, from plumbers to hairdressers, cleaning ladies, auto mechanics, and carpenters, asks for cash under the table. It's an open secret in Toronto that Chinese gangs specialize in black-market electronic goods; Vietnamese in illicit drugs; aboriginals in bootleg booze, and formerly smokes; the American mafia in smuggled gasoline. Then there are the Russian mafia and other central Europeans who specialize in defrauding our health, welfare, and pension systems.

What makes all this cheating worse is that the culprits are also evading income taxes by hiding their income. Sometimes they also indulge in entitlements fraud — working for cash under the table while receiving unemployment insurance benefits, welfare, workers' compensation, or disability pensions. This triple whammy of evasion and entitlements fraud is playing havoc with government budgets. Says Perry: "Governments in the past few years have been uniformly unable to come up with credible budget projections because of the evasion and avoidance."

THE CHEATS

It was spring 1994 in a trendy Italian restaurant in Toronto, and the middleman was explaining to me how he makes a fortune helping Canadians with cash-generating businesses evade taxation. It's called "swaps." It costs the country billions in lost tax revenues, and it will never be stopped, here or elsewhere.

It is no secret that individuals or private companies with cash businesses — notably restaurants or retail outlets of any kind — routinely evade taxes by skimming the till for cash. But swaps allow them to do what drug dealers and smugglers have done for years.

"I match up someone with lots of cash to get rid of with a Chinese immigrant, either just arriving or who's been here for a while," said the middleman. For instance, a retailer with $500,000 in cash will swap his money for a certified cheque from a Chinese immigrant made out to him for $450,000. The cheque can then be deposited in any number of secrecy havens around the world well beyond the reach of the tax man. He can visit his money regularly to withdraw cash to spend or bring home, or he can repatriate it by telling Revenue Canada officials it's an inheritance, which is non-taxable. The immigrant has the inconvenience of carrying a lot of cash, but gets $500,000 for $450,000 by helping the Canadian evade. The middleman gets a fee from both parties.

"That's the favourite trick of the Koreans and Chinese. They have all inherited loads of money, but all they do is hire someone like me or else just take a suitcase of cash home or with relatives regularly, then just bring it back, saying their rich uncle died," he said.

Rich retailers aren't the only ones involved in such shenanigans. The middle class is on the take, too. While most are employed and have income taxes deducted from their paycheques, thousands of Canadians spend more than 181 days per year living illegally in the United States, Mexico, or other lower-cost jurisdictions but pop back home for physicals and free prescription drugs, or to pick up their pension cheques. Some are paying taxes on their incomes, but many are evaders.

Retirees Joe and Jean are Mr. and Mrs. Canada, but they are tax evaders. Born in Canada, he was a middle-management type in an oil company in Calgary and retired with a tidy nest egg. The house in Calgary was fully paid for, and they had a second home across the U.S. border, in Montana, a few hours' drive away. The town they live in has become a Canadian tax-evasion enclave, as have small towns dotted all along the U.S.–Canada border from Paradise Valley, Washington, to Lewiston, New York. Hundreds of thousands more live farther afield, in sunnier regions such as Florida, Arizona, Mexico, the Caribbean, or Europe. Those who live fewer than 181 days per year out of Canada are tax avoiders. Those who live outside the country more days than that are indulging in tax evasion, a Criminal Code offence that is rarely prosecuted.

Joe and Jean are evaders, along with thousands of others, because they live twelve months a year a few hundred miles south, in Montana. "Our two kids live in the house in Calgary, where our pension cheques and other mail goes," explained Joe. "But we live in our house in Montana and travel a lot in the U.S. We go home once in a while to get our annual check-ups and see the kids. But we live in the U.S. because we have so much more disposable income by living there."

Joe and Jean are tax evaders twice. The Americans could slap them with a "substantial presence test." If it showed that they are in residence in the United States six months or more a year, they could be considered residents for tax purposes. Those so deemed have their health benefits in Canada nullified, and retirees would find themselves having to fork out some $4,000 a year per person for partial medical coverage — if they qualified. Those with poor health records or those who are over sixty-five years of age might find it pricier, or unaffordable altogether.

Joe and Jean and others like them may not realize that, since 1992, there has been a compulsory reporting system in place for Canadian visitors. Or they might ignore that, as most do, and are difficult to catch because they have a Canadian address, and their border crossings go unrecorded by border officials.

Joe and Jean are also, of course, tax evaders from the point of view of Revenue Canada because they live outside the country for more than 181 days per year. That makes them non-residents for tax purposes, which is a good-news/bad-news status. The good news is that they don't have to pay Canadian income taxes on any income earned outside the country. The bad news is that they forfeit medical and other social program benefits, and all their worldly assets, apart from their principal residence in Canada, would be immediately subject to capital-gains taxes — a deemed disposition in light of their departure. To boot, as foreigners their estates face punitive American death duties of up to 90 per cent on any assets worth more than $60,000. Another negative is that the American tax system is the world's toughest and most vigilant. Anyone opting for permanent tax status there must pay income taxes on his or her worldwide income.

People who live outside the country cheat Canada's tax base of billions of dollars. They pay income taxes on their pensions and other Canadian income, but pay neither consumer nor excise taxes. Most significantly, their exodus means that, instead of providing work for the younger Canadians who are paying their pensions and medical entitlements, they pay for goods and services from Americans, Bahamians, Mexicans, or others.

The cost to Canada is huge. Some Florida experts calculate that Canadian snowbirds, and other tourists, bring $7 billion a year to the sunshine state. Arizona, California, Hawaii, and Mexico enjoy similar windfalls, and so do the border towns which play host to tax evaders like Joe and Jean from Calgary.

The federal government has never monitored, much less measured, this destructive, but understandable, phenomenon. Official figures in 1993 show that the Canadian government mails 100,000 pension benefit cheques worth $25 million per month to former residents: some 47,898 in the United States; 15,180 in Italy; 9,061 in the United Kingdom; 6,180 in Portugal; 3,534 in Greece; 2,304 in Germany; 1,484 in The Netherlands; 1,368 in Australia; and another 1,500 to Spain and Austria. The figures did not include the hundreds of thousands whose pensions are transferred electronically directly into their bank accounts abroad. Nor did it indicate how many, like Joe and Jean, have their cheques forwarded to them from their Canadian residence.

There is absolutely no foolproof way — except by dramatically lowering taxes — that governments can stem the tax avoidance, tax evasion, and cancerous growth of the underground economy. Canada is in a precarious position. The world's longest undefended border, which we share with the United States, is a gigantic sieve through which contraband, cash, and tax anarchists pass hourly with total impunity. But cross-border shopping, retirement south of the border, and smuggling are only part of the problem. Criminal ruses such as swaps, hiding assets, and over- or underinvoicing strategies can evade millions in a crack.

TAX ANARCHY WORLDWIDE

Money by the billions flows through the tidy pastel-painted stucco office buildings in sleepy Hamilton, Bermuda. Like the lime which cleanses rainwater from the islands' steep rooftops, Bermuda's banking, unit trust, and insurance industry washes the taxes out of the world's capital. There are dozens of tax havens like Bermuda, some with secrecy laws to boot. But Bermuda's spectacular beauty and its situation off the coast of North Carolina make it the home-of-convenience to scads of corporations and to individual Canadians, Britons, and Europeans. Like Canada's biggest family fortune, the Irving empire carved out of New Brunswick, many reside here part-time and legally avoid taxes.

Canadian residents must declare their worldwide income and pay taxes on it unless they have paid the same amount of taxes elsewhere in a jurisdiction recognized by a Canadian tax treaty. Canadian corporations can repatriate dividends from offshore corporations, which is appropriate. Otherwise, Canada would not have any multinational head offices.

But increasing numbers of Canadians are salting away their capital in any one of a number of secrecy and tax havens. A Bank of Nova Scotia report in 1994 noted that, in 1993, some $7 billion worth of "unaccounted for capital" left Canada, compared with preceding years when the figure was only $700 million. The increase is the result of capital flight as Canadians place their funds offshore, legally or otherwise.

Canadians are cheating more than ever, said Canadian-born Saul Froomkin, former attorney general of Bermuda and now a partner with local law firm Mellow, Hollis, James & Martin in Hamilton. His job as attorney general back in 1985 was to clean up the island and rid it of money laundering and dirty money. He did, and Bermuda now has an impeccable reputation. Of course, the action moved elsewhere, to up-start havens such as Tortola or Turks and Caicos, where ill-gotten gains can be easily deposited then transferred anywhere around the world.

As an expert on money laundering and fraud, Froomkin said there is a marked change of late attributable to excessively high taxes in the world's industrialized countries like Canada. "The amount of dirty money is worse than before. Traditionally, it was derived from narcotics or big-time fraudsters. What the world is getting into now are big-time tax exiles and tax evasion.

"People in huge numbers are hiding money offshore because they feel overburdened or feel so unfairly treated that they think there is no point in keeping their money captive at home. What's happening is that high tax rates in Canada and elsewhere are turning what used to be hard-working, honest businessmen into tax evaders. I don't know firsthand, but the feeling I get from Canadians and certain island institutions is that they are getting a lot of Canadian money invested outside Canada which is not there legitimately," he said. "This is not only a money drain but a brain drain. People in Canada and elsewhere are tired of supporting a bunch of ne'er-do-wells. They earned their money the hard way.

"The problem is you can't replace that very easily. This is smart money. A tax system must recognize people will pay what they feel is fair and, if they don't feel it is fair, they will leave or become cheats," he said. "And when the public has no respect for the government, there is mass disobedience."

This is an international problem, he added. "The dirty-money capitals are British Virgin Islands, Tortola, Netherlands Antilles, and Turks and Caicos. The British government has a task force studying this in the Caribbean. And external pressure led to the closure of 300 banks in Montserrat over money laundering. The problem is that industrialized countries are losing their tax bases and criminals are setting up Mickey Mouse offshore banking centres. Then the narco-launderers and big fraudsters get control over the banks and the governments themselves."

The answer is not a crackdown — no such thing is possible. Sovereign nations can pass any legislation they wish. In fact, many developed countries tolerate tax evasion because they have banks that are proscribed from divulging, or asking for, information from depositors. Notable among them are Switzerland, the Channel Islands and Isle of Man, Luxembourg, Liechtenstein, Monte Carlo, Hong Kong, the Cook Islands, Panama, and most of the Caribbean. In Austria, banks are allowed to issue passbooks for accounts whose funds are payable to the "bearer of the passbook." In other words, anyone in possession of the passbook can withdraw funds from the account, which means the identity of the recipient, as well as the depositor, remains hidden.

Besides, an enormous industry has sprung up to facilitate laundering or legitimate tax avoidance. Tax partners in large Canadian, British, or American firms "shop jurisdictions," setting up offshore shelters, trusts, or corporations for multi-nationals or wealthy individuals to avoid, not evade, taxation. Of course, some are outright crooks, including many who advertise in the classified section of large-circulation Canadian newspapers.

"The answer," says Froomkin, "is to make cheating not worth while. If people can pay reasonable taxes and continue to make money, they will pay taxes. Governments must keep their taxpayers happy, but they continue to drive them away," he said. As a Bermudian citizen, Froomkin pays no income taxes whatsoever, only consumption taxes.

"I have no firsthand knowledge about Canadians leaving or hiding assets, but the attorney general's office here advertised in a Canadian newspaper for lawyers and got a flood of sixty applicants. It's nice living in a tax haven," he said.

Getting around taxes is easy, and there are many practition-ers to show people the way. I interviewed one in his Toronto office who explained how it all works. He prefers the Nether-lands Antilles, where the population is mostly white and stable, the electronic communications world-class, and the secrecy laws inviolate. Some other "secrecy" jurisdictions like Bermuda or the Bahamas have cooperated with American tax authorities in the past, in high-profile drug cases. The prime consideration is the cost involved in evading taxes, he said. To set up a corporate shell in the Turks and Caicos costs up to US$8,000, and the annual maintenance fees, US$3,700 per year. The Cayman Islands is cheaper, at US$3,000 for set-up and US$1,850 per year maintenance, but there have been breaches involving Canadian bank branches there in the 1980s, he noted. "Best value is the Antilles, where it's a US$2,600 set-up and $1,025 per year."

The tax dodger does not even need to go to the haven but can get an intermediary to incorporate an Antilles corporation. Shares are placed in the hands of local trustees, but the real owner — the tax dodger — gets warrants to buy the shares held by trustees plus a letter from them attesting that he or she is the beneficial owner. The warrant gives the real owner the right to buy shares of the corporation at a nominal price.

The real owner cannot be a signing officer, non-signing officer, employee, or director. Because his only connection is a warrant, he can truthfully tell Revenue Canada authorities who ask him if he has offshore holdings that he does not have any association with, or "own," a corporation or assets off-shore. The corporation can then open a bank account and stock-brokerage trading account anywhere in the world, except where taxes are being evaded.

"The Antilles has no tax on capital gains, 2.5 per cent income tax on dividends and interest up to $56,000, and 3 per cent tax on interest income after that amount," he said. "You never pay taxes unless you repatriate the funds to Canada. You can buy stock, take delivery of the actual stock certificates themselves to hold in Canada. The certificates are made out to the offshore corporation, but the beneficial [real] owner also gets a power of attorney from the corporation's trustees in the Antilles, which allows him to sell the corporate securities he possesses. That way you disconnect ownership from possession."

Cheats with offshore outfits can also pull off "transfer

pricing" or "over/under invoicing" scams. These are used widely to launder money out of Latin America. "Underinvoicing" works this way: an individual in Canada sells to an offshore vehicle some goods worth $200 for only $100. The prior agreement is that the offshore vehicle will sell the goods for $200, pay no taxes offshore on its $100 profit, and set it aside, or keep it, for the individual in Canada. "Overinvoicing" is the opposite. An individual in Canada buys $100 worth of goods for $200 and his overpayment is kept hidden offshore.

CONFESSIONS OF A TAX ANARCHIST

Alex Doulis is a third-generation Canadian who thinks it is the patriotic duty of every single Canadian to deprive the government of as much revenue as possible. "This is because they waste it, and supporting them is like giving dope to a junkie. As long as they have money, they'll have the power," he said.

Doulis made millions in Canada but does not pay a dime in taxes. He is not a tax evader, but a tax avoider, as are millions of others around the world. Called "PTs," or "perpetual travellers," they salt their money away in the world's tax havens, become non-residents of their homeland for tax purposes, and live anywhere they want for short periods of time. Doulis and his wife live on a yacht in the Mediterranean during the winter months and commute between Florida and Canada in the summer. He's written a book called *Take Your Money and Run* — a book of advice on how to avoid taxes for the rest of your life.

"I left Canada in 1989 because I began to feel powerless. I could not influence the direction of my life, which was increasingly in the hands of the Government of Canada. And the government was deaf. The problem with Canada is it has responsible government, not representative government. I was giving them immense amounts of money, and they used it to perpetuate their power so they don't have to listen to me. They were responsible for me. They did not have to represent me."

Most tax exiles are at or near retirement age. But by age 50, Doulis had made a fortune on Bay Street as a mining analyst with Gordon Securities Inc. and decided to get out. Like 50 per cent of Canadians, he could easily acquire another passport — in his case, Greek, because his father was a Greek immigrant. This also gave him European Union citizenship but, much more important, he choose Greece because that country does not require its citizens to report offshore income.

He left Canada permanently. This process involved turning in his club memberships, selling his principal residence, handing in his driver's licence, and notifying Revenue Canada of his intentions. Exiles cannot stay more than 181 days in Canada. Doulis took all his capital with him and paid a one-time capital-gains tax on the entire value of his assets minus the value of his principal residence. Another option would have been to leave all assets or companies behind in Canada. Those companies would continue to pay applicable taxes on their income and capital gains in Canada. But the owner — living happily ever after in a tax haven — would never pay a dime of income tax on dividends or on capital gains upon his or her death when they flowed from the Canadian company to him offshore. This is what the late K.C. Irving did. He left Canada, as did E.P. Taylor, on the day capital-gains taxes were introduced in Canada — on January 1, 1972. Capital-gains taxes apply upon the death of a taxpayer, and the entire estate, except for the permanent residence, and is between 30 and 40 per cent of the value in taxes.

Canadians need not renounce their citizenship to avoid paying taxes on offshore income, as Americans must. But they must become non-residents for tax purposes. This requirement is why K.C. Irving's will in 1994 stipulated that his three sons must live permanently in Bermuda in order to gain control over the Bermudian trust that owns the Irving empire in Canada. If they were to become trustees as Canadian residents, they would incur taxes on dividends and capital gains upon death, which could cost billions and force the liquidation of the empire.

Canadian tax rules match those in most industrialized countries. The United States is the only country in the world that taxes citizens on the basis of citizenship, irrespective of residency. Americans living in Canada, for instance, must file annual tax returns on their Canadian-earned income. They are credited with the taxes they paid to Canadian governments, but if Canadian taxes paid are lower than the taxes would have been south of the border, they must remit the difference.

Europeans have the same rules Canadians face, which is why Doulis says there are also many Europeans "PTs." "There are rarely Americans, because they consider paying taxes their obligation. But they also don't have onerous taxes. Similarly, Brits pay taxes because they live in a tax haven [top income tax rates are 40 per cent, compared with 57 per cent in some parts of Canada]. But the Belgians and French and many others don't pay tax," he said. In fact, Belgian postal authorities routinely open and read mail coming to Belgians from Caribbean and other tax havens because evasion is so widespread.

Being a tax exile isn't for most of us. Doulis misses friends and things about Canada. So do others, like Laidlaw Inc.'s Michael DeGroote, who went to Bermuda a few years back after selling out. "Mike and I and others sit around in

Bermuda and have a few beers regularly and we all miss Canada, desperately. We really do miss it and I'm considering coming home," said a wealthy Bermudian broker, formerly a Canadian resident.

Another disincentive to leave is the reaction of friends and family. Doulis said some people are envious or hostile. "When I told my friends that I was going to leave for good and for tax reasons, they looked at me like I was some robber baron, raping the country and then leaving," he said. "But I've written my book so that Canadians know their options, and I'm going to promote it as a patriot. Our governments have failed in their duty to the electorate, and Canadians should rise up against the government. This responsibility to rise up against governments interfering with our lives and futures is written into the United States' constitution, but not Canada's. Here we have a colonial-style government that makes decisions for us and ignores us because we are inept."

Doulis blames two decades of concern about Quebec by Quebec-born prime ministers for the current debt mess. "All we've ever heard is 'Elect me. I'm a friend of Quebec.' You never heard a politician — until Ralph Klein and Reform — saying, 'Elect me. I'm a friend of the budget.'"

It took more than one generation of bad fiscal managers to bring the country to its knees, he said. "Nobody understood the economy of Canada. We had trees and nickel, which profited a few. But the trees got further and further away from the mills, and nothing replaced them as an economic activity. Same with mining. In 1969, 22 per cent of the Toronto Stock Exchange's value was mining stocks. Now only 9 per cent is. Then, in 1972 to 1976, Trudeau began running watershed deficits. The resources couldn't pay the bills.

"So there was less and less tax base and more people coming

in, so it was only natural we would have 11 per cent unemployment. The people who I feel sorry for are the kids. It upsets me to see kids defeated on the day they leave college. To see university grads pumping gas and waiting on tables, taking jobs away from kids without an education in Regent's Park or poor neighbourhoods," he said.

The country drifts toward cataclysm. "Then change will occur and be gut-wrenching, horrendous. We will have panic, currency controls, capital controls, restriction of civil liberties. Restrictions on money. And when you restrict money you restrict power and freedom. It's like putting people in jail. Well, I'm not going to be put in jail by Canadian politicians.

"My prognosis is that Quebec will separate and a free-trade agreement bring Quebec in. This blow will be very sobering to Ottawa, but in the long term it will be good for the country. I don't think Canada will continue in the way we know it now. But with the right leader, Canadians will make the sacrifices," he said.

A NATIONAL TRAGEDY

I lined up an interview with Frank Stronach, founder of Magna Inc., in January 1994. We had lunch to talk about his company and its impressive turn-around, as well as public policy in Canada. Stronach sought to run as a Liberal party candidate in 1989 in a bid to become leader, but lost. He remains, however, a keen observer of Canadian politics.

But soon into our talk, he floored me when he said he had essentially left Canada for good and would operate Magna's global financial and strategic headquarters from Zurich. This move was partially to take advantage of the

European opportunities, but it was also because he had given up on Canada.

"I think we have four years at the most to correct Canada's basic flaws. If we do not, I see a major breakdown in social order. The fact is that Canada's taxes must be lower than the United States'. Canada relies on foreign capital, and we're not far off from the point of no return when we cannot repay the debt. Taxes must go higher, social spending must be axed, and this will chase more businesses away. The business tax base is eroding already," he said.

"I have actually moved already," he said, "but I will be here once every two months or so." Just turned sixty-one years of age, Stronach is not retiring to ski or clip Magna coupons in Switzerland. He is setting up Magna's global strategy and financial headquarters in Zurich. He said it was to take advantage of technology, but he's slowly withdrawing the company in order that it may maximize its competitiveness through lower taxes and be where the action is. Canada is no longer a good place to "grow" transnational corporations.

By contrast, Swiss personal tax rates are only 30 per cent. "Corporate income taxes in Switzerland are negotiable," he said. "The government sat down with me and said, 'You're our customer,' and that was its attitude."

This refreshing approach is why, along with its fiscal rectitude, Switzerland is probably the world's most successful nation. Stronach's plans are to leave Magna's North American headquarters in Toronto. But future large-scale growth must be in Europe, the United States, or Latin America.

Stronach's departure is a national tragedy. Many of Canada's most prominent tycoons are gradually withdrawing or leaving altogether. They can save taxes by leaving, but would put up with higher rates if they did not feel that Canada is a sinking ship. Magna remains in Canada, but the loss of an entrepreneurial genius like Stronach means fewer jobs, fewer exports, and fewer revenue-producing initiatives.

Canada has become a lousy place to do business. Governments here treat enterprises like cash cows and instruments of public policy rather than as customers. They confiscate, bully, overregulate, overtax, and heap social responsibilities onto the backs of business. Then they wonder why their tax base disappears, and people like Frank Stronach leave for good.

Although Switzerland is one of the most attractive countries in which to live and do business, it is not, as some might think, a nasty, unenlightened Third World tax haven. Switzerland has a social safety net that makes Canada's look as stingy as Brazil's. For starters, some 50 per cent of Swiss live in public housing because real estate is so expensive. The Swiss enjoy cradle-to-grave benefits in health, education, and welfare. Its farmers are the world's most subsidized, and its GDP per capita is the world's highest.

The Swiss can do this because they have never provided social services that they could not afford. They never asked businesses or workers to pay higher taxes than were paid in neighbouring countries. Meanwhile, Canadians pay more taxes for fewer social services than the Swiss enjoy and — to make matters worse — our kids and grandchildren will be on the hook for our debts.

THE EXODUS

"If you have money in Canada, why dig a foundation, buy machinery, build a building, and cope with regulations?" Frank Stronach asked me. "You are better off buying government bonds than investing in bricks and machinery. Everyone sucks off the system, from welfare recipients to lawyers. Nobody wants to make things or get their hands dirty. Everybody wants to be an accountant or a lawyer and wear a suit. This is not wealth creation."

Little wonder then that a survey in 1993 revealed that the majority of businesses would move to another country, notably the United States, if they could. This is sheer greed, say union leaders and socialists. But that's not the case. It's survival because, in the world's integrated economy, lower taxes and less red tape can be more important competitive advantages than low wages.

Canada's small businesses and corporations choke on regulations and compliance costs. Not only do governments spend money enforcing regulations and collecting taxes, but their bureaucracies impose costs on doing business that few people outside the business community fully grasp. There are dozens of forms to fill in annually; complicated mandated payroll deductions to collect and remit; accounting and legal requirements, environmental, labour and health restrictions; building codes; severance and fringe benefit issues to resolve; human rights, pay equity, and employment equity matters. These hassles and expenses provide a rationale for many to leave Canada, or to cheat while staying here.

But bigger companies are captives of the system, and while the government has tried to keep their taxes competitive they are still higher than rates imposed in the United States. While personal income taxes on average nearly tripled between 1981–82 and 1992–93, corporate income taxes increased by only 30 per cent, to $14.7 billion from $11.79 billion. Despite complaints from unions, New Democrats, and Liberals, corporate tax hikes could not parallel personal tax hikes because that would have accelerated the departure of businesses from Canada.

In a global economy, governments have little control over corporate tax rates. This is why in Europe — where personal taxes are higher than Canada's — corporate taxes are lower. Canada's corporate income taxes are equivalent to 2.5 per cent of GDP, below the OECD average of 2.9 per cent. Unfortunately they are still higher than in the United States, which is the only comparison that truly counts.

Tax advantages, if large, and combined with other advantages, have caused thousands of companies and individuals to move south. No one knows how many, because few leave in the glare of publicity, as did Varity Corporation, formerly Massey-Ferguson Limited, which shuffled off to Buffalo in 1991. But moving head offices is just one aspect of the leaching away of Canadian business to more favourable environments. Virtually every Canadian company with U.S. operations or markets has been legally shifting divisional headquarters or profit centres south to pay lower corporate, property, and business taxes.

There is a worrisome outflow of capital too. For instance, Canada's gigantic mining industry — still a major engine of economic growth — has been slowly abandoning Canada for years. In 1993, miners spent more money exploring in tiny Chile than they spent in all of Canada. The country's largest, American Barrick Resources, did not spend a nickel on Canadian exploration.

A friend who is an executive with one of Canada's largest transnational companies, and a household word, spent most of 1992 and 1993 flying around the United States to move four dozen divisional headquarters there. "We are moving every possible operation because our competitors pay lower

32

taxes and we have to in order to compete against them," he said.

Taxes strangle enterprise and incentives in Canada, said Harvard professor Michael Porter in his 1991 study for the Business Council of National Issues in Ottawa, "Canada at the Crossroads: The Reality of a New Competitive Environment." He said taxes were diminishing whatever competitive advantages Canada enjoys. "Combined federal and provincial government debt has been growing more quickly than the economy for a decade," he pointed out. "Governments in Canada have often had a detrimental effect on the competitiveness of Canadian industries. High taxes can reduce the willingness of talented individuals to work hard, upgrade skills, take risks and even remain in Canada. A broad social safety net may have reduced incentives to expend greater effort or upgrade skills. Governments held the view that ample resources would continue to exist to fund social needs. This led to chronic public sector deficits which have contributed to higher inflation, interest rates and taxes."

Unable to change the system, Canadians like Tor Boswick with Mid-Ocean Investments in Bermuda leave Canada and set up shop abroad to help others do the same. "Canada is heading inexorably for bankruptcy," he says. He has observed a flood of interest among well-heeled Canadians who want out. "Individuals are the ultimate source of wealth, and economic growth only occurs if people are allowed to better themselves by taking chances and keeping the rewards," he said. "That's not the case in Canada any longer." Individuals without huge wealth are also leaving. David Perry said, "I have two friends who can work by modem from the Caribbean and moved last year. One moved for tax reasons, and the other as a matter of principle."

Taxes aren't the only reason for the exodus of business. Anti-business regimes and economically illiterate governments are driving jobs out of the country. Decisions such as the one that shut down mining forever in the Windy Craggy area of British Columbia after mining companies had found ore bodies and spent tens of millions of dollars exploring in good faith was a "Canada Shut for Business" message heard around the world. As *The Economist* magazine noted in 1993: "Canada's mining reserves are huge and yet between 1986 and 1991 the country failed to attract a single new mining project worth more than $250 million. The number of smaller projects in Canada fell by 14 per cent but doubled in Australia."

Other Canadians are legitimately sending their hard-earned cash elsewhere to work for them. In 1993, Canadians bought more stocks and bonds outside the country than ever before, increasing their investment to $13 billion from $3 billion in 1990. By 1994, some 40 per cent of the value of all retail portfolios in large brokerage firms were invested in U.S. or other foreign securities. Only 20 per cent of RRSPs, pension funds, and life insurance company holdings can be invested abroad. If Canada were to lift these currency controls, the money would undoubtedly pour out.

THE LESSONS OF VARITY

The history of Massey-Ferguson Limited — forerunner of Varity Corporation — is a frightening metaphor for Canada's future. Massey was Canada's biggest entry into the world's manufacturing sweepstakes. In the postwar years, it had become one of the three worldwide giants in the tractor and combines business. The company had operations in sixty countries, and tens of thousands of employees turning out state-of-the-art agricultural machinery.

Unfortunately, Massey-Ferguson became controlled by a holding company called Argus Corporation, run by two tight-fisted tax anarchists — E.P. Taylor and Bud McDougald. The two controlled Massey-Ferguson, along with many other assets, by holding a mere toehold of just 11 per cent of shares. Their stewardship was disgraceful: Massey was starved of equity infusions because the Argus group did not want to put up fresh cash or to sell new shares to others, which would have diluted their 11 per cent holding. So the company borrowed money to expand or do research. Debts piled up until the market for agricultural implements fell through the floor, along with commodities prices, in the 1970s. Massey-Ferguson became a casualty.

By the time heavy weather hit in 1980, Argus was controlled by Conrad Black, and the company's CEO was a witty Briton named Victor Rice. A financial whiz, Rice had been transferred to Canada years before from Massey's large Perkins Engines division in the United Kingdom. Black walked away, giving Argus shares to Massey's pension funds. Rice, a capable leader, singlehandedly steered the company through near-bankruptcy, got governments to backstop his debt, convinced banks to restructure and stretch out loan repayments, pruned, undertook debt-for-share swaps, and turned it into a highly profitable auto parts and tractor company.

Then he did the unthinkable. He decided to move the headquarters to Buffalo, New York, for good. This departure was another example of Canada's deteriorating economic prospects. Varity's new headquarters in Buffalo, New York, is in an handsome mansion, surrounded by iron gates and beautiful lawns, and protected by security guards. It's a classy oasis in an otherwise mundane, rust-belt city. Across the street is a derelict Howard Johnson's Restaurant. Nearby are other huge mansions which fetch one-quarter the price mansions in Toronto go for, even after the collapse of real estate values in the early 1990s. Rice said his Buffalo home cost US$540,000 and would have cost $4 million in Toronto. Groceries are 35 per cent less, as are other living expenses, from airplane flights to cabs, vacations, and consumer goods.

"Our operating costs for the headquarters are 35 per cent less. The increase in our personal purchasing power is dramatic. But that's not the reason we moved the company," said Rice. "We moved for a number of reasons. Most important and overwhelming was that we would never become recognized in Canada as the revamped company we had become. We also were not noticed or followed much by American investors and analysts in the United States, even though we had been interlisted for forty years on the New York Stock Exchange. Americans don't care about Canadian companies, and Canadians don't care about Canadian manufacturing companies for the most part."

Rice brought Massey-Ferguson through the delicate, and dangerous, negotiations with governments and banks, and by 1990 had 350 million shares outstanding — stock issued to rescuers in return for converting loans or fresh capital. Then he and his team set about downsizing the tractor business and acquired some exciting auto parts companies in the United States. Slowly the company was being transformed into an American company, assets-wise, but the stock languished at around $1.50 per share, despite improved earnings. Rice decided to do a "reverse split" to get the value of the stock up in order to get noticed. He was also concerned because shares trading under $5 apiece cannot, by law, be bought by big institutional investors, such as pension plans, so the big investors don't bother following their progress. Rice decided to offer a swap of one share for every ten held. "But the Toronto Stock Exchange would not allow us to do that unless we changed the name of the company in order to avoid investor confusion," he said. "But we had already changed the name from Massey-Ferguson to Varity to avoid stigma." So Rice felt that his efforts to enhance Varity's image and value were being frustrated by unnecessary regulation. At the same time, he was being harassed by negative publicity in the Canadian media. "We were referred to every day it seemed as 'Varity, formerly the financially troubled Massey-Ferguson,' even though the company was doing well. We had lots of baggage despite the name change," he said. "So we were fleeing that heritage."

Buffalo was chosen over Chicago, which was near its auto parts plants, only because it was close to Toronto so that his Canadian executives and their families would have the option of living in Canada. "But none of them do because, contrary to Canadian opinion, Buffalo and the States are a wonderful and interesting place to live. Canadians have a great deal of arrogance about the crime rate and so on, but Toronto is getting just as bad," he said. "As things turned out, I realize that Canadians are supremely arrogant as to how much better their country is because of the American crime, guns, social apartheid, and all those negatives. But that is totally beside the point. The United States in the last fifty years has been the greatest job creator of small businesses of any country in the world. It's millions and millions. And that's given them the highest living standards."

Rice received death threats from some Canadians who considered the move "treasonous." The company's stock after the split, however, settled at $15 per share. Once it was an "American" company, analysts and investors began to follow and invest in it. "Ten shares worth $1.50 four years ago, or $15 in total, would now, after the split and increases in share prices, be worth US$50 a share. This company is now listed as 127th in the Fortune 500, mentioned in *Businessweek*, followed by important newsletters or stock gurus, and taps into an equity market of 250 million people. This company could have been bought four years ago for $100 million and now has a market capitalization value of US$2 billion," he said.

When asked if he felt guilty about taking the company's headquarters south after all that government help and money, Rice responded: "No, I don't. My job is to do my best for the shareholders, and this move has certainly paid off. No one [in government] ever asked me whether Massey-Ferguson should have been bailed out. It should not have been because of the cost."

Varity isn't the company Massey-Ferguson once was. When he became CEO of Massey in 1980, the company had 68,000 employees worldwide. Now it has 14,000 because it sold off most of its traditional tractor-producing businesses and got into smaller, more profitable enterprises. What has happened to this company merely points out that good stewardship is often missing in Canada, both governmentally and corporately, while the U.S. system breeds, and feeds on, success. Varity was an outcast in Canada and could not interest shareholders. Once it crossed the border, Americans backed a winner and turned it into a smash hit. It's no different from what happens to Canadian actors. The unfortunate reality is that to make it really big you must go south of the border. This was always the case, but taxes have made departure more imperative. And this is Canada's tragedy.

RIPPING OFF
THE TAXPAYERS

ILL JAMES IS A SUCCESSFUL CANADIAN BUSINESSMAN whose wife works at home raising their four children. She had not filed an income tax return for several years because she was not employed and had no taxable income. But the couple filed jointly because, technically, she was a "dependant" for tax purposes.

At the end of 1992, she got a notice from Revenue Canada suggesting she file a separate 1991 short tax form. She was told she was eligible to receive from the government a sizeable amount of money — which turned out to be $370.25 a month. Because she had no reported income and had been noted on the old baby bonus scheme as the mother of four children, reasoned the bureaucracy, she "qualified" for a child tax benefit.

The point is that she was a dependant, and the family was extremely well off. So the couple ignored the notice. "Just a few weeks later," Bill James told me in an interview, "a Child Tax Benefit notice was sent to my wife, telling her that she's eligible for a child tax benefit of $370.25 a month based on four children for the first six months of 1993. They went on to say that 'if we reassess your 1991 tax return we'll adjust the amount and send you an explanation.'"

Here was another example of Canada's bureaucrats firing off cheques that no one had either asked for or proved entitlement to. No investigation was conducted to establish the claim's validity. As James told me, Revenue Canada had his wife's social insurance number and, within its own department, could have cross-referenced the number to the couple's jointly filed income tax return, which would have shown that they had ample income.

This story underscores the three myths that support Canada's elaborate social safety programs. The first myth is that the recent levels of spending are necessary because poverty is widespread in Canada. The second myth is that help is distributed to those who really need it. The third — and most economically crippling — myth is the notion that Canadians are basically honest people. This naïve belief has spawned a distribution system for social payments that is based on the honour system. And while I would agree that most Canadians, or human beings for that matter, are basically honest, Canada is plagued by as many immoral, desperate, ruthless, or shiftless people as any nation. Canadians are not a superior race.

As for poverty and targeting to the needy, Mrs. James's story is a good example of the incompetent and naïve way the federal and other governments distribute "help." The lack of homework or proper research which the bureaucracy applied to her case is also a good example of why this country has a social safety net that it can no longer afford. Even though the Jameses stopped payment of the cheques, Mrs. James would still be considered — by government computers that measure only reported income for tax purposes — to be living below the poverty line. Lobbyists for so-called poverty groups would include Mrs. James as one of Canada's "poor" people.

The National Council of Welfare reported in the early 1990s that 4 million Canadians, including a million children, lived in poverty. This was based on a poverty-line income for a family of four ranging from $13,644 in Quebec and $14,704 in Prince Edward Island, to $15,159 in Alberta and $17,078 in Ontario. The flawed assumption underlying this analysis is that income reported for tax purposes is the same as actual income. That is just not true, especially since the explosive growth in the underground economy and other forms of tax evasion.

For instance, counted as poor folks are all the country's university or post-secondary college students who happen to file income tax returns for a summer or part-time job. In 1993–94, there were 585,200 registered, full-time university students; 328,447 part-time; and 365,060 post-secondary college students. What is misleading about including them as impoverished is that their incomes are low by definition. Like Mrs. James, they can't be making money because they are engaged in non-remunerative activities — attending school and doing homework. But their low income is certainly not a sign of poverty; if they aren't supporting themselves, then they are being supported by their parents or families, or are independently well-off.

By the National Council of Welfare's definition, a retired millionaire from Hong Kong I know would also be counted as poor. He hides most of his assets and income outside the country and declares only a tiny income. So would an unethical businessman who writes off everything to eliminate income for tax purposes, and a fisherman in Nova Scotia whose accountant

splits his income among his wife and all five kids. Also supposedly poor are pensioners who have houses and other real estate
fully paid for, but a small income from a portfolio of capital
gains, dividends, or tax-sheltered instruments and pensions.

The GST rebate is another annoying example of waste. To
fend off cries from poverty groups that the tax was regressive
and hurt the poor, the timid Tories decided to give those below
the poverty line a quarterly GST rebate. This is an across-the-
board cheque sent tax-free to those kicked out of Revenue
Canada's computer. Before becoming Trade minister, Liberal
Roy MacLaren told me that his son, who worked summers in
Toronto but attended Cambridge University in England the
rest of the year, was getting his $45 cheque every three months
from the Government of Canada. So do virtually all the
country's students, together with many millionaires without
"income" and on and on.

Despite such facts, lobbyists and New Democrats routinely
and ignorantly cite the low reported taxable income from
well-heeled students and hundreds of thousands of others as
proof that free enterprise exploits and excludes "millions."
Canada's social safety net cannot shrink, they say, and should
be expanded.

Canada has not, of course, eradicated poverty. But the
figures — based, as they are, only on reported taxable income
— are dramatically lower than trumpeted by special-interest
groups and New Democrats. So-called poverty rates are
mostly fiction. So is the notion that help is going where it is
really needed. These are all myths derived from naïve book-
keeping, a naïve bureaucracy, and a naïve media that neglect to
analyse the statements and figures from poverty lobbies.

While the fact that poverty in Canada is often exaggerated
is good news on one level, the bad news is that the myths are

crippling the country. Tens of billions of dollars' worth of unneeded health, welfare, workers' compensation, pension, family allowance, and other benefits are handed out indiscriminately, without investigation or follow-up, to people who neither need nor deserve help.

And as Mrs. James's case demonstrates, even when information is easily obtained, the administration of these programs is so poor that too much is handed out too often to many who don't need it. This has encouraged a gigantic underground of cheats, which, in turn, has undermined taxpayers' trust in the way the country is run, thus encouraging flight, more cheating, and tax evasion.

As taxpayers revolt, governments borrow even more abroad and run up interest payments on a frightening scale. The whole area of social programs must be reinvented if the dangerous debt situation is ever to be solved. In 1994 alone, taxpayers will have forked out $16 billion for welfare and $61 billion for health care. Workers, employers, and taxpayers will contribute $19 billion in annual unemployment insurance benefits, and employers $6 billion in workers' compensation payments. This adds up to $102 billion, more than Canadian governments spend on anything else.

CANADA'S POVERTY MYTHS

Most provinces, with help from municipal and federal taxes, pay families of four on welfare assistance as much as $5,000 a year more than the so-called poverty-level income. Similarly, unemployment insurance, pension supplements, rent subsidies, and a host of other expensive social expenditures are based on the incorrect impression that Canada is overrun by

4 million very impoverished people. This is bad arithmetic and bad social policy.

The Fraser Institute published an important book in 1992 called *Poverty in Canada*, written by Christopher Sarlo. "In Canada's context, poverty simply means being less well off than most other people," Sarlo wrote. "There is an exaggeration of the cost of true necessities and 'poverty' is more a matter of social inadequacy than economic inadequacy."

By far, the biggest problem is that the "poverty" figures have no basis in reality. The national poverty figures are based only on taxable and reported income, and not on the other sources of support or subsidy that people live on. Sarlo pointed out that, in 1988–89, roughly 37 per cent of post-secondary students lived at home with parents, and 63 per cent lived independently, with the majority unmarried. Categorized as "unattached individuals" living below the poverty line, they are considered too poor to afford all the basic requirements of living. The point is, support from parents and family loans are not counted as income because these infusions are not reported as taxable income — perhaps because they are not taxable, or because they are taxable and recipients want to hide the income.

Besides constituting incorrect addition, the government figures are misleading because they don't break down how many "impoverished" individuals are self-employed persons whose income is as understated as possible to avoid taxes on profits, who are reporting losses from earlier years, or who are forgoing salary or draw in order to build up their business by reinvesting their capital.

Others report low incomes to Revenue Canada for a variety of reasons having nothing to do with impoverishment. Some 250,000 immigrants come to Canada annually, and many arrive partway through the taxation year. Half of Canada's marriages end in divorce, which means that, by definition, every year tens of thousands of couples suddenly find their income drastically reduced. They are not poor. They are divorced and living on less income as family units. Others in the category of low income who are not poor are Canadians who return home from abroad during the year; those leaving the country during the year; and those being released from prisons or mental institutions in mid-year (30,000 mental patients are released per annum after more than a thirty-day stay). Each of these cases has nothing to do with poverty. For many, their low reported income simply means that, for whatever personal reasons, they earned less than usual that year.

Another category lumped into the mix as "poor" is made up of those who make a conscious decision to accept a low income, either temporarily or permanently. In this group are artists, musicians, actors, writers, and others who must invest years of free labour before breaking into their chosen professions. Then there are religious people, volunteers, members of sects or cults who, in essence, have taken a "vow of poverty."

Besides all of that, there are those members of the underground economy who hide all or part of their income. This would include waiters, cabbies, hairdressers, barbers, restaurateurs, retailers, tradesmen, fishermen, and farmers. In fact, farmers in this country have hoodwinked politicians about their income level for years. The average farm income is low because so much barter and contra take place. It's also low because living costs on a farm, where food is readily available, are usually very low. So are housing costs, which are written off as a business expense. The result is that farmers operating enterprises with $1 million or more in assets have gotten more hand-outs and concessions than any other special-interest group, and as undeservedly as others.

Another case of bad information concerns the Old Age Security Supplements, some $4.7 billion of top-up entitlements to so-called impoverished seniors. Again this is a case of mediocre management because seniors are allowed to deduct depreciation from their income for the purposes of qualifying for the supplement. As one *Financial Post* reader in Quebec explained: "I own an apartment building worth $400,000 and I can get a supplement because I write off the depreciation against my income. The forms ask seniors to declare all their income then show net rentals after depreciation and everything else — taxes, expenses. I write $6,000 off my taxes for depreciation but then the government lets me get the supplement even though the depreciation isn't really a cash outflow. It's ridiculous."

Still, the poverty professionals like the Social Planning Council of Metro Toronto successfully mislead and manipulate the media and politicians. The council, for instance, estimated in the late 1980s that 200,000 "Ontario families were homeless and caught in the cycle of poverty," according to Sarlo. These people were not actually without a roof over their heads. Two hundred thousand was the council's best guess as to the number of people living in substandard or unaffordable housing. They defined "unaffordable" as shelter costing more than 50 per cent of someone's reported income. So the poverty propagandists equated housing problems (some of which are chosen freely by people or are inflated because of hidden income) with homelessness.

True homelessness in Canada is mostly a mental illness, not a socio-economic issue. Those hundreds who sleep on grates or park benches are mentally dysfunctional, alcoholics, or addicts. Help is available if they can be convinced by police or skid-row social workers to seek it. As a director of the Clarke

Institute of Psychiatry, I know that mentally disturbed street people are treated for thirty days or more, given medicine to arrest their hallucinations or other symptoms, and then released into halfway homes with social-worker support systems in place. But often they stop taking their medicine because they are not forced to take it, or because they feel "cured," and then the voices or hallucinations begin again and they return to the streets. This cycle is repeated, and outside the support structure provided by a mental institution, the victim eventually dies of an overdose, exposure, or starvation.

Another meaningless, much-touted symptom of poverty in Canada is the food bank. While these are run by well-meaning persons, the fact was that, until I wrote about it, they never screened recipients to ensure that they were on assistance or truly needed the provisions. It was common knowledge, I wrote, among university students that, by parking their cars a short distance away and "dressing down," they could pick up about $100 worth of groceries from a food bank two or three times in one day. That way they'd have more money left over for beer, movies, or eating out. Now some food banks ask for a welfare card, which, by the way, proves very little because it carries no photograph of the bearer.

Poverty exists among those who are chronically unemployed, disabled, or dysfunctional economically or psychologically. But even when taxpayers are asked to help the truly needy, governments have no idea how much is really needed or to what extent the families and relatives of the needy should be enlisted to help out.

Welfare, pension, or family allowance workers routinely hand out cash without regard to such important factors as "unreported income," wrote Sarlo. "In 1988, 550,000 households headed by someone 65 years of age or more were considered 'poor.' Of those, almost half — or 250,000 — owned a home. Of those, 90 per cent were mortgage free."

Canada's social safety net managers don't calculate the value of free housing but would give those 250,000 old folks the Old Age Security Supplement, even though they own their homes and therefore have lower living costs than other seniors. These lower costs are not taken into consideration in the case of seniors or others either. Sarlo wrote: "In 1988, 44 per cent of families with total reported income of less than $15,000 were homeowners, 72 per cent of whom were mortgage-free. And yet 23 per cent of mortgage-free homeowners were considered poor, earning less than half the average income."

This points out another fallacy in our poverty figures — people who have conducted their affairs in such a way that their living costs are very low do not have to work full-time or make huge amounts of money. So there is absolutely no necessity for the rest of us to interfere with the choices they have made freely or to support them.

Another unreported income benefit not included in government calculations is the huge subsidy enjoyed by Canadians who live in the country's 700,000 "social" or public-housing units. "A single mother in British Columbia with two kids and an income $10,500 is considered $500 below the poverty line but if the value of her social housing unit is taken into consideration she is $2,500 above the poverty line," Sarlo reported.

Worst of all, entitlements are often handed out irrespective of the differences in living costs from region to region. A house or apartment in Newfoundland costs a fraction of what comparable housing costs in British Columbia or Ontario, which is why it's not unusual to find third-generation homeowners living in entitlements in Newfoundland. They have no incentive to move or to work.

A three-bedroom bungalow cost an average of $92,900 in fall 1988 in St. John's, Newfoundland; $84,000 in Fredericton; $67,000 in Trois-Rivières; $89,000 in Regina; and $79,000 in Kelowna. Average monthly rents in six-plex apartment buildings for units with two bedrooms also varied: $523 per month in Calgary; $490 in Regina; $596 in Toronto; $631 in Vancouver; $370 in Trois-Rivières; and $515 in St. John's. Rents in small towns were considerably cheaper, another factor also never taken into consideration in terms of the dole. In 1988, rents for two-bedroom apartments in towns with fewer than 49,999 people ranged from $385 in Newfoundland to $345 in Quebec, $454 in Ontario, $434 in Saskatchewan, and $365 in otherwise pricey British Columbia.

Sarlo's point is a strong one. These disparities are rarely taken properly into consideration when cost-of-living increases, supplements, or special subsidies are being calculated. Neither is the fact that the so-called averages are not paid by many Canadians. When doling out help, Ottawa has a Toronto bias and consistently exaggerates true housing costs paid nationally. Sarlo wrote: "In 1986, 54 per cent of Canadian tenants paid gross rent of $400 per month and 10 per cent paid less than $200 a month. In 1986, 24 per cent of all homeowners had housing costs of less than $200 per month; another 30 per cent had costs of only $200 to $400 per month. So for more than half of Canadian households, shelter costs were less than $4,800 in 1986.

"This country's self-styled social reformers would have us believe that poverty is Canada's major problem. But three to five million Canadians are not poor. Traditionally, poverty means real deprivation, of someone lacking basic needs in such a way as to compromise long term physical health," said Sarlo. "That is not the case in Canada."

In terms of reported income only, Canada's distribution of wealth hasn't changed a great deal since the 1950s — proof by social engineers that our system is not doing enough to help the "poor." But, as Sarlo points out: "Once money income is adjusted for such factors as under-reporting, benefits-in-kind, education, capital gains, potential additional earnings and taxes, the distribution of income is compressed [no extremes top and bottom]."

Huge economic inequality is a big myth in Canada. Even if it were true, it would not be intrinsically unjust. It is the result of human experience and genetics. Life is a bell-shaped curve. There are winners and losers: the brilliant and the dim; the fast and the slow; the energetic and the lazy; the ambitious and the shiftless. That is why egalitarian societies do not work. In the last attempt to create one, the former Soviet empire, the cream, or ruthless, always rose to the top, earned more money, and enjoyed more privileges than the rest. Enlightened societies should be meritocratic to encourage socially acceptable wealth creation. Governments should skim just enough taxes from the rich to run things and to redistribute to the truly needy in a sensible way.

THE BIGGEST MYTH OF ALL

Even if Canada had four million "poor," there is no way the country could afford the amount of help now given. But gutting social programs, as must be done, involves attacking the so-called sacred trust which many politicians feel is the very essence of the country. By examining this argument, one can see how misguided it is.

Answer this: If parents cannot afford to send their brightest youngsters to Harvard, does that make them inadequate parents? If parents suddenly hit hard times and must cut their children's allowances, does that make them terrible parents? If a child cannot afford to pay $100,000 so that his or her father can get a quadruple bypass from the best surgeon in the world, does that make the child ungrateful and rotten?

The point is that parenting, like governing, is much, much more than a fancy house, three-car garage, private golf club membership, big allowance, designer clothes, and prestigious private school education. Good parenting is teaching children to respect the rights of others, to care for and help others, to cooperate and share. Being a good parent is not spoiling your children with material goods or hand-outs by running up debts.

By the same token, Canada is not inadequate because it cannot afford its current level of spending on health, education, unemployment, pension, and welfare entitlements. Nor is Canada a superior country for spending so much so unwisely with borrowed money.

Canada's governments will spend about $70 billion more than they collected in taxes in 1994. That is more than $1 billion a week, roughly $140 million a day, $6 million an hour, or about $1,667 per second. In order for Canada to have the wealth to pay for that amount of entitlements, the country would have to have another thirty Hemlo mines, dozens more $2-billion Ford Motor Company plants employing tens of thousands more Canadians, and another ten oil megaprojects.

"We decided that we don't have a revenue problem, we have a spending problem," said Alberta premier Ralph Klein, the best political leader in Canada's recent history.

What is this "sacred trust" that requires a nation to live beyond its means until its industries are crippled by taxes and it goes bankrupt? The actual fact is that those who talk of a "sacred trust" have a strictly materialistic view of Canada, as does a child who dislikes his parents because they cannot afford to give him everything he wants.

Canadians never asked for these give-aways. Canadians believe in the country, sacred trust or no, and those who stay do so because of friends, safety, political stability, and the many benefits Canada offers. Those who are constantly moaning about insufficient social spending, or resisting reforms to a system riddled with fraud, treat Canada as some kind of rich daddy who can manufacture money at will. They are spoiled.

But universality — underpinned by the "sacred trust" sacred cow — insists that rich people deserve tax-free pensions, free medical benefits, and free prescription drugs when they retire. Canada's social safety net insisted until 1993 that anyone who quit a good job deserved unemployment insurance benefits. Canada insists that the rest of us pay for a woman who has chosen to have a child so she can take a holiday for up to nine months with pay. Canada insists that snowbirds living in cheap countries deserve to have the rest of us pay their medical costs.

Canada insists that the economically privileged class, whose children take the lion's share of post-secondary education places, be subsidized by those whose children go no farther than high school. Canada feels that people with high incomes deserve to live in rent-controlled apartments and still get first-class services. In 1993, the Reform Party estimated that some $22 billion worth of social entitlements were handed out to families whose incomes were above an income of $53,900 a year. We're going broke financing our myths and believing in a "sacred trust" that nobody in their right mind would sub-scribe to, given the realities. Canada's social spending will eventually hurt those it was meant to help.

THE GREAT CANADIAN RIP-OFF

In 1989 I realized that Canada's social safety net was an issue, not of excessive generosity, but of criminal abuse — because of the massive potential for fraud that is built into the system. So I spent the next few years writing dozens of articles exposing problems and crusading against abuses and bureaucratic or political ignorance. During that time, I've been picketed by poverty organizations, called "irresponsible," a "redneck," "neo-Nazi," "heartless bitch," "liar," and worse. I take most of this abuse as an indication of a job well done. But I take especial pride in the names used and denials uttered over the years by New Democrat ministers in Ontario and British Columbia. Ministers in Ontario claimed that my stories were bogus. A British Columbia cabinet minister accused me of "irresponsible journalism." But, by 1994, both governments were admitting that fraud was rampant and trying to set up systems to combat the abuse. Unfortunately, their actions may be too little, too late. The sophisticated underground that has sprung up to defraud the system is a cancer that may never be fully removed. And the billions of dollars that governments have squandered through their dreadful governance have added to the horrid debt burden Canadians shoulder.

At a gasoline station in downtown Toronto, a man with a sandwich-board paced in front of motorists. The sign read "Good SINs here half-price." He was peddling bona fide social insurance numbers for $200 apiece. He also had health cards available, he told me, "but I don't want to advertise that one."

Business was brisk on his corner, and the man, also receiving welfare at the time, confessed to a $200-a-day tax-free income, thanks to entitlements fraud. Equally telling was a news story in 1993 which mostly went unnoticed, except by me. Fraud thieves had broken into a motor vehicle licensing office in Toronto and made off with driver's licence blanks and the machines that photograph drivers. Strange? Not if you want to create false identification documents in order to get welfare, health cards, or social insurance cards. Police tell me health cards fetch $3,000 and up in U.S. border towns where pregnant women who are HIV-positive snap them up so they can have the child in Canada. The ensuing benefits are generous, to say the least, because any child born in Canada becomes a Canadian citizen entitled to get free medical coverage forever. About eighteen AIDS victims per month defraud their way into Ontario, according to a secret health study leaked to me in August 1993. Their medicine, called AZT, costs taxpayers $5,200 a year alone.

My welfare exposés began when a young man named "Steve" called me after I had written about health care frauds involving drug addicts, U.S. treatment centres, and prescriptions. He said welfare fraud was rampant and that he, personally, was doing it "because all the immigrants and refugees are doing it." It was a shabby rationalization, but his story was important, if only to make officials realize the attitudes out there and the ease with which the system could be beaten. He said he knew people receiving multiple cheques, and that he "lent" his address to others in return for 10 per cent of their welfare payments. He also said he used his welfare prescription drug card to get prescriptions from many doctors every month for tranquillizers like Valium and narcotics or amphetamines for resale on the black market.

Bob Rae's cabinet ministers accused me of making Steve up, but the story pushed a public hot button. Spurred on by Steve's story, I worked out that tax-free welfare payments were equivalent to as much as $35,000 a year for a family of four. I wrote that in a column, and Ontario social services offices — and *The Financial Post* and *Toronto Sun* switchboards — were flooded with thousands of protest calls within days. The minister of Social Services had to temporarily hook up twelve phones and information officers to answer calls. The minister's remarks attacked me and disputed my figures. Three years later, that same Bob Rae government announced a crackdown on welfare fraud.

The new initiative met resistance from the usual left-wing critics who are fond of quoting that ancient socialist icon, the late David Lewis, on the issue of welfare fraud. "He called it 'peanut-sized' crime," civil liberties lawyer Alan Borovoy told me during a television show. It was an irrelevant, bankrupt remark. The "peanuts" were now $16 billion a year nationally and growing malignantly.

After "Steve" the scammer, I heard from "Joyce," an irate welfare case worker who was tired of the hand-outs and abuses. She documented how Ontario had created North America's first welfare-on-demand jurisdiction. Home visits were forbidden. Benefits had soared so that recipients made considerably more than the case workers who handed out the money. Even youths under eighteen years of age who were living at home could get welfare if they left or if their parents said they didn't want to support them any more. She also said there were no computerized systems, so that a crafty recipient theoretically could obtain benefits from all the province's offices. That was still the case in 1994. So was the fact that welfare recipients could also be getting workers' compensation, disability, family allowance, unemployment insurance, or pensions at the same time. No one checks.

An example of the slapdash give-away involved Mrs. X and her husband, both elderly pensioners whose name and address were used by a ring of welfare fraudsters. Mrs. X, urged on by a welfare worker, told me her story, but was frightened to have her name published. The scam was simple and involved welfare recipients who claim they are moving apartments in order to get the first and last months' rent up front. These rent cheques are made out to the landlord, but the recipients supply the "landlord's" name. Often the supposed landlords are accomplices or relatives. But, sometimes, the scam artists use phoney addresses and names.

"We began by getting cheques from welfare made out to us every month," said Mrs. X. "I called the police and they said at least seven people on welfare got first and last months' rent up front, then cashed the cheque somewhere. Then their monthly welfare rent cheques began to arrive at our house. They never picked up those cheques because they were long gone after they got the first and last months' rent. This was fraud because we have never rented out anything to anybody. We were told another case involved thirty-five cheques sent to one address each month."

A Toronto welfare worker — who met with me secretly because workers in the province were told not to talk to me — said things still had not changed two years later, in 1994. Cheques for first and last months' rent are still routinely handed out without double-checking. Then regular cheques are sent out. "They can cash the first and last months' rent cheque even though it is made out to the landlord. They just endorse it; the fake landlord doesn't even know because he's not expecting the cheque. All that's required is a landlord's letter or signed Promise of Address form, but these are easily forged. Workers often call the landlord, but don't check whether the phone number matches the address. Recently, a pay phone number was given, so the welfare worker just got an accomplice on the phone because she was told he was only available at a certain time. If workers are suspicious they are not allowed to report matters to police because they are told: 'It's not worth it because amounts are so small.'"

As is true for welfare payments, offices never check with one another to see if the first-and-last-month scam is being pulled off elsewhere. Problem is, the crooks know enough to use phoney documents and identities in each office or to change the birthdate on their drivers' licences — the principal means of cross-referencing. Cheque-cashing street bankers will also facilitate the lost-welfare-cheque scam by refusing to identify the person who cashed the cheques in return for a high fee. It works this way: welfare recipients report their cheques lost or stolen; they are immediately issued replacements in the same amount; and they cash both.

Another annoying scam involved rental allowance increases requested by welfare recipients. A worker said one welfare recipient, living with his mother, told his welfare worker that his mother had "doubled" his rent and he therefore needed twice his monthly rental allowance. But if a fellow is living with his parents, why should taxpayers contribute anything toward his rent? Why shouldn't his family be forced to help?

The irony, according to the social worker, is that the New Democrats imposed strict 4 per cent rent controls, but were not concerned about huge rent hikes if the payee was themselves, the government, to a welfare recipient's "landlord." My articles created a firestorm of controversy in the province. Others began to look for signs of what I was talking about, and they found them. Stories about this or that ring of fraudsters began to appear in newspapers across the country.

In 1993, a Southern Ontario city council meeting exploded when it learned that the town was supporting a community of nearly 700 teenagers who had taken advantage of Bob Rae's welfare rules. They had left home and were being comfortably supported in townhouses by taxpayers. The teenage welfare payments are also a problem because the children are supposed to attend school regularly once they leave home, but their welfare case workers are not allowed to see attendance reports from the schools.

Another story, in March 1994, involved a federal audit of the Micmac Indian Band in Big Cover, New Brunswick, where there had been a large increase in welfare costs over four years. Welfare payments jumped 70 per cent in that time, easily outpacing population growth. Members of the 2,000-member band were getting a staggering $6.3 million a year, compared with $3.70 million just three years before. What had happened was that sympathetic native social workers were labelling short-term unemployed aboriginals as "unemployables" to help them get more money. It worked. They also got huge shelter allowances. Of course, on top of all that, treaty Indians in Canada pay taxes of no kind, and fish, hunt, and farm without restriction.

Another region where natives and others were ripping off the system was in Thunder Bay, where a local alderman, Evelyn Dodds, called me for information and leads. I gave her an earful and she went to work. Large-scale arrests for welfare fraud occurred in Thunder Bay in spring 1994. Dodds came up with plenty more information about rip-offs contained in a brief which she sent to me.

"Fraud is rampant but if fraud is reported the hearing could take six months to schedule and the guilty parties are still getting the money while that is happening. It is a very simple matter for people to establish multiple addresses and to access welfare from multiple jurisdictions simultaneously," she wrote. "In Thunder Bay, we have had examples of people collecting welfare who were also collecting from smaller northern towns, from native reserves, from Manitoba, or from neighbouring townships. Some 200 out of the 320 delivery sites are not automated and 20 per cent of caseloads are from non-automated sites."

She noted that it is difficult to prove that people were cohabiting illegally, and obtaining fraudulently family allowance entitlements, which are for single-parent families. Another problem was that landlords readily provided false rent receipts and that fraudsters were using cheap apartments as mail drops for cheques from different agencies. Some rent receipts have been signed by non-existent people and detected only by checking tax rolls. But this was time-consuming.

Even if fraudsters were caught, the crown attorneys were ill prepared, and courts were so slow that some accused simply skipped town. Another difficulty was that witnesses at cases often could not testify because they could not afford the lost wages and babysitting costs that they would incur by attending proceedings. Some were intimidated.

Even when convicted, guilty parties were still able to get future benefits. The overpayments were sometimes so large that they could never be repaid, and fraudsters routinely referred to them as "interest-free loans" from the government. Repayments could not be more than 5 per cent of benefits, so if large amounts were stolen there were, in actual fact, no consequences. As for Bob Rae's rules allowing sixteen- to eighteen-year-olds to leave home and go on welfare, Dodds said this was "irresistible" and had the effect of encouraging immature rebellion and irresponsible behaviour.

Thunder Bay officials also discovered that many social benefits recipients had not filed income tax returns for years; that chasing husbands for support payments was not allowed without the permission of the mother; and that applicants could falsely claim to be supporting children who were actually being supported by other relatives. This was easy to pull off because workers did not do home visits. Another impediment to screening applicants was that workers were not allowed to request income information and to verify whether others were living in a house unless this information was volunteered.

In one lengthy interview in 1993, a British Columbia welfare worker told me that a six-figure overpayment to a recipient over many years was "buried" by the supervisor responsible for it. The worker was forbidden to tell anyone.

"The amount of fraud is unbelievable," she said. "People work full-time and collect assistance. I've got ten or fifteen claimants working full time, and I can't do anything about it. How do I know? I phone them for an appointment and their roommate says, 'He's at work.' Single men are the worst, and immigrants too. They drive up to our office in their landscapers' or plumbers' vans and workclothes to collect their cheques."

She said some clients drive Mercedeses and live in beautiful houses. "Your home and car are exempt in terms of determining what assets you have and whether you need help," she explained. There is no double-checking of marital status, number of children, documents, age, or rents. She said her office opens twenty-five new files daily, and each of its eleven caseworkers is allowed to make only six home-inspection visits per month.

"There have been other harmful changes by the New Democrats. Under the Socreds, when your youngest child turned six months, you were required to look for work, and day care was available. Now, under the NDP, you don't have to look for work until your youngest child is nineteen."

Bob Rae went one better in Ontario. Single parents never have to work if they don't want to, even when they are dumping their kids off at day-care centres. Governments in Canada have gone beyond helping families in need to financing needless and harmful intervention.

THE REFUGEE RIP-OFF

The biggest consumers of Canada's welfare system have been its "refugees." In Canada and elsewhere, a well-organized immigration industry has sprung up which encourages fraud on a massive scale. My first inkling that this was criminal in nature came in 1989 when I noticed that the "boiler-room boys" who touted fraudulent stocks during the 1980s had shifted to providing immigration services. One brochure I obtained out of Amsterdam boasted that anyone with $250,000 could become a Canadian citizen within four months. Perhaps that was possible — but only through fraudulent or criminal means. Perhaps the fraudsters would simply take the $250,000 and never deliver.

But, whatever the scam, it was my first evidence that there was an industry devoted to getting our passport and citizenship privileges. And why not? People wanted to escape collapsing economies or dictatorships and enjoy the good life in countries like Canada. To boot, our social safety net is so generous that it actually contributed to the flow of illegals because our system of automatically handing out entitlements provides a nifty way to pay immigration consultants or smugglers for getting you into Canada. Once in the country, refugees who can't pay cash up front can sign over welfare cheques, in whole or in part, to their smugglers. This is not possible in the United

States, where refugees are given a haven, but no help, until their hearings are held. Most U.S. refugees disappear into previously arranged jobs in illegal sweat shops or turn to criminal activity to survive. Some never show for their refugee-status hearings, and no one knows how many are at large.

In other words, we are financing their ability to sneak or defraud their way into Canada.

The smugglers have different nicknames, depending upon which part of the world they are from. "Shleppers" help central and eastern Europeans get into western Europe or Canada; "coyotes" assist Latin Americans for fees; and "snakeheads," Asians. The most lucrative, and easiest, technique has been to declare "refugee" status.

Under the Geneva Convention, Canada and other wealthy countries agreed that anyone declaring him or herself a "political refugee" once inside their borders would be completely looked after. They would be deported only if an investigation determined that they were lying.

The idea was a sound one — that the world's wealthiest would harbour victims from abusive regimes that had driven them out. Unfortunately, Canada and others have done an abysmal job of screening refugee claimants. Many "refugees" are not fleeing tyranny but are economic asylum seekers, jumping immigration queues and getting financial support to do it. More than 500,000 "refugees" flooded into Canada during the 1980s, on top of our heavy immigration levels, putting undue burden on our social programs. Canada's immigration authorities are so incompetent that they have allowed into the country as "refugees" people from countries where there is not even trouble. In one notorious case in Ontario, officials let a woman from Iran stay in Canada as a "refugee" because she claimed her husband beat her up. Even convicted criminals and a handful of murderers already in Canadian prisons have been granted the right to request refugee status. Immigrant or refugee criminals should be deported immediately after conviction.

Enormous controversy in 1994 followed the cold-blooded murder in a restaurant of a twenty-one-year-old Toronto woman. Two of the men were from Jamaica, and one had convinced Canadian officials not to deport him after several run-ins with police. They said he could stay unless he misbehaved.

But Canada has played host to hundreds of thousands of bogus "refugees," giving them welfare plus health, education, and housing benefits from the moment they land. One deluge — 25,000 or so Somalians consisting of warlords and other members of the élite from the losing side in that civil war — will contribute very little, if anything, to Canada in the future. "Their children are very violent in the school yard and come to classes without underwear or any knowledge of how to use cutlery or toilets," complained a public school teacher whose school has been totally disrupted by these invading hordes.

A Buffalo newspaper revealed that the wife of a murderous Somali warlord was living on welfare in public housing in London, Ontario, with her four children. Hardly a refugee fleeing for safety, the woman had returned several times to visit her husband with the result that she became pregnant once again. Her last child was born in Canada, which ensures that she and her children can never be deported. Worse yet, that Canadian child will allow her to "sponsor in" her husband and dozens of relatives under the family unification program. Deportation proceedings had been launched in early 1994, but without tough new legislation and a change to the Citizenship Act, she will almost certainly beat the system. In fact, virtually all the 10,000 refugees who have been ordered deported had, by spring 1994, been allowed to stay on humanitarian grounds.

It is notable, and unfortunate, that by 1994, two or three years after the Somalis staged their mass invasion of Canada's welfare state, most are still on assistance but work for cash under the table, according to Toronto police. One bank teller in the formerly Slavic "Junction" area of Toronto now overrun with Somalis tells some horror stories.

"One woman came in with that veil over her face. She was married to a Somali but was an Anglo-Saxon Canadian woman. She was cashing in her welfare cheque, but had another bank account with $25,000 in it from the sale of a store she and her husband ran until the end of 1993. I'm sure they never declared the income from their convenience store either, but they used to deposit thousands in cash every week. They withdrew it to buy a house," she said.

Getting "refugees" into Canada is simple. Smugglers coach them carefully as to what to say and what they are entitled to once in Canada. All these Somalis had to do was buy return trip air tickets from anywhere in the world and use fake identification so that the name on the boarding pass isn't theirs. Once on board the plane, the smugglers collect or destroy the fake passports. This is so that fraud cannot be proven. Once in Canada, each says the magic "refugee" word and is automatically given entitlements plus a free lawyer under legal aid to stickhandle him or her through the process of establishing the right to stay in Canada. Their lawyers often help them concoct a story about the hardship they endured back home, and they have come up with some cunning strategies.

Other benefits have flowed from the New Democrats who are determined to turn the welfare system into an open-ended negative income tax for the so-called poor. They made massive rule changes in British Columbia and Ontario which amount to welfare-on-demand. They also forbid caseworkers to pursue husbands who refuse to support their wives and children. This rule played nicely into the hands of a Vietnamese couple. Like many people who have lived with brutality, they had become incredibly ruthless. A Vancouver social worker called me in 1993 and related several stories which illustrated the problems.

"I had a Vietnamese guy and his wife come in and ask for welfare because he was being garnisheed hundreds out of his income every month for unpaid VISA bills," she said. "I told them they could not get welfare to repay their VISA bills. So the next week she came in alone and said her husband had left her and the kids, and she demanded welfare for them. She got it, even though the husband had probably not left. But there was no way of checking up. We weren't allowed, and besides it's difficult without enormous expense. And because the NDP said we cannot go after the husband without the wife's permission — and she said we could not do that — we had to give her welfare and could not pursue it any further.

"Refugee claimants come into our offices the same day they arrive and get on welfare. We buy them furniture, groceries, give them apartments, dental work, everything. If you're from China or Guatemala and get in here, you live like a king on welfare. Canadians don't know what's going on. We give them welfare and they also go to food banks and work for cash on the side," she said.

Third World denizens are not the only abusers. One Vancouver welfare worker told me in 1993 that her province handed out welfare to American visitors, even after checking with Immigration and finding out they have no proper status. With welfare come medical, dental, and housing benefits. "I have brought these Americans to the attention of Immigration because the very act of applying for welfare makes you an illegal alien. But nobody at Immigration cared. I asked what their status was. They sent back a form saying the people were visitors. Our policy says we have to pay. We have quite a few on assistance. A lot of gays from San Francisco with AIDS come up here and pretend they are living common law with a friend to get medical coverage," she said.

IMMIGRANT FRAUD

"Kathleen" attended an investment seminar I gave in fall 1993, then another in spring 1994. Of Chinese origin, she had immigrated with her parents from Hong Kong around twenty-five years ago. She's a Canadian citizen now and proud of it. She's also a pharmacist and gave me information secretly because she wanted her fellow Canadians to know that many Chinese and other immigrants are ripping off this country's health and welfare system.

"Many immigrants, increasingly from Taiwan, come to Canada, settle their family and the grandparents into a house, and the husband goes back to Hong Kong or Taiwan or the Philippines to make a living," she said. "They do not report their global income on their Canadian tax return — as they are supposed to — but only report their Canadian income, if they have any. This is tax evasion, and Revenue Canada isn't hooked up to Hong Kong tax rolls."

These men are nicknamed "flight husbands" by the Chinese in Canada, and Kathleen suspects most of them don't declare their offshore income. If they do, there's nothing illegal about what they are up to. If they don't, they are tax evaders and costing us all a fortune in schooling and medical costs for their families.

"Just look at the number of frequent flyers that go from Hong Kong to Seattle or San Francisco and back. They arrive in the U.S., drive across the border, and their movements are unrecorded. They go back the same way and there is no policing of this.

"I also get disgusted because many elderly immigrants obtain large quantities of their prescription drugs and take them to their own country. Pharmacare [B.C.'s drug plan] allows them three months' supply at a time, and seniors pay only the dispensing fee. The drugs these seniors take cost hundreds of dollars, and their doctors are in cahoots with them. The seniors also get a pension after ten years and don't actually live [here] — but live with other relatives in the U.S. or Hong Kong — but they sneak across the border like the husbands do. They come to Canada once a year for medical stuff. Their families get three months' supply of drugs for them and mail the drugs to them."

She also said that private schools in Canada catering to foreign Chinese students are sometimes engaged in large-scale tax evasion. Some declare a religious affiliation — which means students can write off fees as donations — but the schools really are not religious. Also interesting, if true, she said the pupils often board with school staffers or in apartments, but their landlords don't declare the rent they get from the kids.

Kathleen also related incidents involving welfare scams: "A couple came in with welfare cards to get free prescription drugs and told me they'd just had a great holiday in Costa Rica. . . . One young lady told me she's on long-term disability and welfare pays for everything. Then she told me she's selling cars. . . . A family swings everyone's prescriptions under the grandmother's name because she's over sixty-five years [old] and gets it free," she said. Kathleen also said it's an open secret that rings of Middle Eastern refugees in West and North Vancouver send "tonnes of insulin" and other drugs under their welfare cards home. A guy came in to have a $100 tranquillizer prescription filled as a welfare recipient. "He wouldn't let me put a label on it. What do you think he's doing with that? He's selling it on the street."

What's sad is that immigrants like Kathleen are becoming the targets of hostility because provincial governments have ignored the fraud, even though my articles have been exposing this for three years.

"An old Caucasian lady said to me recently, 'Go back where you came from. We don't need you in this country!' I turned around and said, 'Madam, this is my country.' That's why I decided to call you and tell you what's going on, because the government must stop it. You must write my story and tell Canadians what's happening. To these Hong Kong and Taiwanese people, we are a laughing stock."

It's bad enough that some legitimately landed immigrants are ripping off the system so badly. But Canada has been deluged with illegal aliens, so-called refugees and immigrants, under the family unification privileges set out in the Immigration Act. This is, simply put, because we are a sucker nation, known as an easy mark by people around the world who make a spectacular living smuggling people into welfare states like Canada.

Immigration officials are easily bribed, with money or sex, and there have been several prosecutions. One businessman told me how Immigration was easily defrauded by those wishing to obtain entrepreneurial or "fast track" residency. The rules are that they must invest large amounts of money and/or buy a business that employs a certain number of

Canadians. One case I reported to authorities involved a businessman in Toronto who "sold" his business several times per month for $200,000 to immigrant hopefuls. The catch was, he "bought" it back simultaneously for $150,000. This allowed him to keep his business but pocket $50,000 for each fraud he helped along. Meanwhile, Immigration accepted the "purchase" agreement without asking whether it was sold back immediately and without follow-up to see whether the new purchaser was actually the proprietor.

Another way to get citizenship quickly was to buy up to $1.2 million in Canadian investments over five years and fulfil the standard two-year residency requirement to get citizenship. But the residency requirement was never monitored, so a prospective citizen would buy or rent a house as an address, drive across the U.S. border, then fly home to work without Immigration's knowledge. Contrary to Canadian tax laws, they would not declare their offshore income for tax purposes, nor would they live at least 181 days per year in Canada to fulfil the residency requirement. Undetected, they would get citizenship, which entitled them, and many relatives, to medical, pension, and other benefits in Canada. To boot, the $1.2 million invested offshore would be declared, but could be kept offshore tax-free for five years if a certain type of trust had been established. Once the five years was up, the new Canadian citizen would have to repatriate the money and pay taxes on the income derived. But, in the meantime, tax-paying Canadians were supporting his health benefits or his children's education.

Another citizenship ploy is to give birth to a child here. I wrote a column about this in January 1993 based on information passed on to me by a disgusted friend. She said her husband (a doctor) had recently seen as a patient a woman in labour who had been brought to him by her "husband," who happened to be an immigrant from Jamaica. The baby was delivered at the taxpayers' expense. But imagine the surprise when it was discovered that the man's "wife" had been brought into the same hospital a year before and had undergone a radical hysterectomy, making it impossible for her to ever have children again.

"We found out he'd passed off his sister from Jamaica as his wife so that the kid could be born here and become an automatic Canadian citizen," explained my friend.

The next step undoubtedly was to claim family allowance and public housing. Instead of being deported, with her child and "husband," for defrauding Canada, she is here forever with her kids and whoever else she can give birth to, or sponsor from Jamaica.

A Vancouver social worker reported to me that "babies of convenience" are born all the time at a hospital near the airport. The pregnant women come as visitors, borrow a relative's health card, have the child, get its passport, then return to Hong Kong, Indonesia, or wherever, and apply for the child, parents, and siblings to immigrate. A Toronto passport officer, of East Indian descent, complained that five or six women per week from Asia were demanding passports for their newborns. "Who paid for the delivery of their child? Why are we letting them do this to us?"

Another awful story involved a Canadian woman who conceived a child as a result of a connubial visit to her American husband in Mississippi, who happened to be serving a life sentence in a U.S. prison. The woman was living with her parents in Canada, had the child free, and will be able to sponsor its father into Canada, if he is ever paroled.

While such cases are relatively rare, family-unification provisions and the flood of elderly immigrants represent one of

Canada's most troublesome, and expensive, immigration issues. For instance, it is appalling that under current immigration laws I could sponsor my retired and prosperous American parents into Canada, where they could get full and complete medical care without ever having contributed a dime in taxes to Canada.

In the United States, by contrast, the parents of Canadian immigrants are given no such privileges. Americans allow families to unify but do not give social assistance of any kind to relatives for ten years. Canada is a different story. Our rules allow Canadian citizens to "sponsor" dozens of immediate relatives, including siblings, grandparents, uncles and aunts, parents, and children. Of the 900,000 immigrants let into Canada from January 1989 to January 1993, 450,000 were brought in under family-unification rules. Of those sponsored in during 1991 and 1992, some 54,000 were more than sixty-five years of age, with half more than seventy years old. Even worse, Canada automatically gives anyone who arrived after age sixty and stayed for ten years Old Age Security.

This is significant, because anyone over sixty-five years of age costs taxpayers four times' more in health care spending than the average of roughly $2,300 for every person. This means the 54,000 immigrants over sixty-five years of age could cost the system $270 million a year alone. If they live for ten years, that adds up to a staggering $2.7 billion. If we have averaged that many seniors over the past five years, then they alone cost the system $1 billion per year.

This is reckless management — to invite unnecessary costs at a time (the early 1990s) when we are closing down 5,000 hospital beds and eliminating 5,000 nursing positions. With the added burden of foreigners to care for, by 2010 Canada will have a 161 per cent increase in people over age eighty-five.

71

That's a formula for financial disaster and guarantees that waiting periods and rationing are imminent. Already the elderly represent 11 per cent of the population, and rack up 40 per cent of costs. In 1987, for example, the elderly used 48 per cent of patient days in general hospitals, 72 per cent of days in long-term facilities, 33 per cent of days in psychiatric hospitals, and 20 per cent of physician services. In Ontario, seniors get free drugs, as in most provinces, and the average cost of prescriptions for seniors there has been growing by 20 per cent a year. Seniors account for only 10 per cent of the province's population, but they ring up 40 per cent of prescription drug sales.

Drugs aside, no one begrudges higher medical costs for the elderly. But we cannot afford to look after the elderly from other countries too.

After my articles about elderly sponsored immigrants I received a letter from Harvey Stark of Vancouver. "As a Canadian visa officer at various embassies for fourteen years, I was struck by the fact that so many sponsored parents and relatives would be an obvious immediate health care problem on arriving in Canada. Many sponsored parents coming from lesser developed countries had grown up without adequate health care and nutrition, and were already old in medical terms at the age of forty or fifty. However, as they were sponsored dependants, we were basically powerless to refuse them even in instances when we knew their children had already made arrangements for them to be admitted to hospital on arrival in Canada. Canada's generous health care system is very well known abroad."

Worse than entitlements costs, sponsored immigrants are no longer really sponsored. All that relatives must do is swear an affidavit that they can no longer support a grandparent or grandchild, and the immigrants are entitled to welfare. It's also not uncommon for immigrants to have their sponsored parents babysit for free and give them a receipt, for tax purposes, so they can write off the expense.

Current rules require returning expatriates to be resident in Canada for three months or so, but no longer, before they qualify for health benefits. That merely means that some advance planning must be done by those who want to come back in order to get "free" medical attention they have not contributed toward for years. Several cases point out the abuses. One Canadian male friend lived happily for a decade in the United States until his kidneys failed. Unable to afford U.S. medical care, he came home and gets daily dialysis. This means Canadian taxpayers are on the hook for a six-figure annual cost indefinitely, which is absolutely free to him.

Another case involved a woman married to a Canadian executive who was transferred and promoted to a new position in Los Angeles. She needed to have a hysterectomy and — because they did not have to surrender their health cards — came back to Toronto to have it done by her old physician at the expense of Canadian taxpayers. A third case involved a friend's sister, born in Canada but a resident of Britain for thirty-five years, whose marriage ended. A diagnosed manic-depressive, she required expensive medication and a place to live. My friend willingly put her sister up but was told by a social worker at a mental hospital that her sister was entitled to welfare and a living allowance each month because of her disability. She applied and received it without question, even though she had never lived in Canada as a taxpaying adult.

Such situations are doubly unfair considering that taxpayers who have contributed to the system all their lives cannot get hip replacements or elective surgery because of rationing. And this situation will simply worsen.

THE GREAT CANADIAN HEALTH RIP-OFF

My first foray into health care fraud started with a phone call from a faithful *Toronto Sun* reader. He said that my stories about snowbirds in Florida racking up excessive and unfair U.S. medical bills were only the tip of an iceberg. A reformed alcoholic himself, he told me about the hundreds of alcoholics and drug addicts from Canada like himself who were routinely going down to fancy, expensive spas in the United States for cures that rarely worked. The price to taxpayers was a staggering $20,000 per month at certain facilities. This included first-class airfare, limousines to and from the airport and treatment centre, and even accommodation for the wife and kids. He gave me a couple of names of places in New Hampshire, so I called to double-check. The operator not only knew their numbers off by heart ("a lot of you Canadians go there, don't you?" she remarked) but volunteered the names of several other popular spots.

That story sparked others and led one addict to go public on the CBC to tell the story of how he had racked up $1 million worth of medical costs travelling over many months from one of these facilities to another. He would go to New England in the summers, and south in the winters. There were even people on commission in Canada to drum up such business, and I learned from a prison warden about cases of addicts who had gone to Paris and London for treatment on the taxpayers' tab. Worse yet, drug treatment facilities began calling to say that health authorities routinely rubber-stamped these requests for offshore treatment without checking to ensure that space was unavailable in the province. Some facilities charging $800 a month were ignored in favour of the hugely expensive American centres.

Fortunately, that nonsense ended in Ontario. Then I turned to other health care rip-offs. I found that health care costs by 1990 had soared to $61.753 billion, or $2,321 per person, and 9.2 per cent of GDP. This was up from 1975, when costs were only $12.267 billion, or $540 per head, and 7.2 per cent of GDP. That whopping increase was bad enough, but I discovered that Canada's health system — like its welfare and immigration systems — was totally mismanaged.

The health mess was no less staggering than welfare's. Health officials had never computerized sufficiently. They had not screened beneficiaries, nor had they created a system that would catch doctor or patient fraud. Besides facilitating out-and-out rip-offs, the system was so poorly designed that ordinary, honest Canadians and physicians could overdemand and overservice without consequences. In 1992 a Liberal plan to issue a health identification card backfired when it was discovered, months after issue, that hundreds of thousands of cards were missing. Quebec went a step farther; following a pilot project, the province issued identification cards with photographs. But this was also inadequate. The only way to eliminate health, welfare, and all entitlement frauds is to issue a "smart" card containing, in a microchip, information about the individual, a fingerprint, photo, and verifiable signature. Privacy considerations are secondary and a red herring. Canadians submit all the time to credit-card, bank, and other intensive forms of scrutiny. And so they should when they have financial dealings with the public sector.

The private sector clearly understands the value of the credit cards it issues. The same cannot be said of the public sector, whose cards, particularly health cards, are at least as valuable as, say, a VISA card. A colleague whose wallet was stolen not long ago got an insight into the difference in valuation.

He called VISA and other credit-card companies, who required that he give them a predesignated codeword (his mother's maiden name is the usual). His credit cards were immediately cancelled. When he phoned Ontario health officials to report the loss of his considerably more valuable health card (there is no limit on a health card), a bureaucrat told him to mail in details and a new card would be sent, by mail, at a later date. This casual approach was wrong for two reasons. First, someone could have rung up thousands of dollars in procedures with it by the time the card was cancelled. Second, the government was taking his word for it, which meant that he could have lied, kept the card, and sold the use of it to someone else.

In 1993, the Ontario government set up a special task force to look into the stories I had been writing about fraud in the health and welfare system. I was leaked a copy of the internal report, which was never supposed to be published. Little wonder. It was a thoroughgoing indictment of the government.

In fact, deputy Health minister Michael Decter was miffed that I had gotten a copy but said, gracefully, that it was "your efforts that brought this all about and you deserve all the credit in the world for that." In 1994, Ontario was finally working on a new "smart" card.

The leaked report estimated that health care fraud in Ontario alone cost taxpayers $980 million a year. That meant $1 out of every $17 was spent unnecessarily. Other highlights shocked even me because of the scale of the losses and waste:

— About 30,000 people in Ontario facing deportation orders were getting health benefits, costing the system $42 million a year.

— Claims have been paid on health cards even though holders have died, because there is no automatic deregistration after death. Claims are paid on cards held by people who have left the province or country.

— An estimated 695,000 people had two health cards, exposing the province to fraud. The report estimated that "registration-related fraud" costs up to $284 million a year. Another 469,500 "questionable registrations" create a potential "exposure" of $657.3 million a year. These are registrations for people who are likely ineligible because they do not officially live here.

— The report recommended coordination with other governments and agencies responsible for welfare, workers' compensation, immigration, and unemployment insurance to stop the massive fraud. This request came because often benefits frauds are related to health frauds. In a chapter called "multiple doctoring," the task force examined twelve cases where health card holders went to an average of twelve different physicians in a year while on welfare. Then, in the section called "Overlapping MCSS [Ministry of Community and Social Services, i.e., welfare] benefits," it is stated that welfare offices do not compare cases. "The MCSS systems appear to have no common identifiers for registering their clients for benefits," said the report. "Estimates of MCSS's exposure to benefit abuse is $1.3 million annually for every 120 MCSS clients." If true, that would amount to another $900 million a year or more in fraudulent entitlements to welfare recipients.

— Another shocking finding was based on a survey of two border towns: it is likely that some 60,000 Americans or U.S. residents have Ontario health cards. This represented a potential cost to Ontario of $84 million a year. If such ineligible claimants had AIDS or cancer, the costs would be astronomical.

— Drug dealers and drug users are having a field day with Canada's health system, both here and in the United States. The report estimated $135 million is paid out for narcotics and other health expenses to "unresolved reference numbers."

The report contained two case-studies. The first involved a male, with one health number but two welfare drug-benefit cards from two different regions — "Mobile throughout Ontario, visiting emergency rooms, walk-in clinics and doctors," said the report. He had prescriptions for tranquillizers and codeine narcotics and various other medicines in August 1993 — a total of $611.02 in drugs and $736.11 in doctors' fees charged in that month. "Subsequent investigation revealed that this patient was not eligible for drug benefits for the month of August."

The report estimated that 14,500 people are fraudulently receiving two or more welfare payments each month.

— Invalid immigration document numbers were another problem. Health officials never sought validation from immigration officials before issuing cards to refugees or immigrants. A random sampling of Ontario's 1.07 million landed immigrants with health cards (W in front of the number) showed supporting documents were rarely required when cards were handed out. Immigration document numbers were not checked, even when there was an easy formula to do so. Of 731 numbers checked, 190 were incorrect.

"There is evidence that a large proportion of these numbers are erroneous and there also appears to be a significant risk of inappropriate health coverage assigned to thousands of temporary persons in Ontario, it concluded.

— In a section called "Frequent Births Analysis," the report confirmed that incidents like my Jamaican childbirth story had occurred. "One case had claims from one woman for two deliveries in two separate hospitals in Kingston and Richmond Hill one day apart. Another case had claims paid for two deliveries one month apart for a single woman. These services were performed by different doctors in the same hospital in Kingston. She was also admitted to the Peterborough Hospital at the same time as admitted into Kingston."

There were four more "suspicious cases where claims were paid for two deliveries performed at the same hospital to the same woman just two and four months apart," it said.

— Doctors are likely defrauding the system too. "Eighty-nine physicians billed for the same delivery more than once. One physician billed the ministry twice for services on 19 different occasions. While most duplicate billings were not paid, the ministry still paid 14 of 139 duplicate claim items."

— Ontario had 87,213 "refugees" with health cards. Only 7 per cent presented supporting documents to prove they were refugees. Of this 7 per cent, nearly 10 per cent had document numbers that, when checked, proved to be phoney or incorrect. Of those 93 per cent who never showed extra documents, researchers found that the refugee registration numbers of 4,970, or 5.7 per cent, were fake or wrong.

— Canadians who live abroad can prearrange medical coverage. Of seventy-nine persons who made huge claims while living abroad, only two had received permission to keep coverage, and yet all claimants were paid. "One person was approved at a cost of $700 per day up to a total of $210,000. The other person was treated for psychotherapy at $596 per day. Many other examples exist where a client arrives in Ontario, applies for a health number and then immediately incurs major medical claims."

— Most disturbing was evidence that AIDS victims were entering Canada without trouble, even though they were ineligible. In one month, the special AIDS code was added to twenty-seven health cards within thirty days of the cardholder's first acquiring his or her card. Of those twenty-seven cardholders, eleven were citizens, nine were newborns, four were immigrants, two were welfare clients, and one was a temporary resident. Six of them had arrived in Ontario a month earlier from the United States. Many had border addresses, and officials never verified whether they really lived in Canada or not.

"There would be added incentive for a [pregnant female] U.S. resident to deliver in Ontario and register for a health number if the mother tested positive for the HIV virus. AIDS drugs cost $5,200 a year. Based on our sample, if 18 suspect registrations occurred in the month of July 1992 — and all were participants in such a drug program — this would cost $93,600 per year for these new registrations in drug costs alone. If there are 18 per month, then drug costs alone could be $1.12 million per year," the report concluded.

Canada's health care system is plagued by fraud, overservicing by doctors, and overdemand by patients. On average, twelve prescriptions are issued each year to every Canadian man, woman, and child. An average of $250 worth of doctors' fees are run up. Those of us who go to the doctor once a year and get one prescription annually are paying for people who must go dozens of times a year and get hundreds of dollars' worth of drugs.

THE WORKERS' COMPENSATION RIP-OFF

These plans were a good idea in the beginning, except that they are run by governments who seem unable to manage anything responsibly. Workers' compensation is an insurance scheme, paid for by employers in the form of a payroll tax. Premiums are based on wages, type of work, and the number of past claims. The system allows an injured worker to get up to 90 per cent of his or her salary if disabled as a result of a work-related injury. At least, that was the idea. Now everything from stress to injuries sustained while playing in a company hockey league or while in the car on the way to work is considered a legitimate claim. Before money is paid, the worker's injuries are supposed to be verified by a physician, and the employer is also asked about the accident or problem.

These plans are administered by the provinces separately, but, as with anything governments do, they have paid out considerably more claims to more people for more questionable reasons over the years. The result is "unfunded liabilities" collectively of nearly $15 billion. In other words, given current claims and current premiums paid, that is what the shortfall amounts to. Unfortunately, workers' compensation premiums in Ontario, for instance, are the highest in North America, and so is the unfunded liability. Once again, it doesn't seem to matter how much money is handed over to governments: it is never enough.

In spring 1993, I got a call from a high-ranking official at Ontario's Workers' Compensation after I had written a few critical articles. He was defensive at first, and then told me a horror story about Ontario's scheme and how he suspected that the mafia, both Italian and Russian, were defrauding some $500 million of the $3 billion handed out each year.

When the story appeared, all hell broke loose. The New Democrats went into denial again, the opposition pummelled them, and attempts were made to assassinate my character, but remedies were finally set in motion. My informant suspected that organized criminals had set up phoney doctors, phoney pharmacies, phoney patients, and phoney employers to get claims. He said some of the country's most notorious gangsters received workers' compensation and that the money involved was so huge that Canadian health investigators, doctors, physiotherapists, pharmacists, and inspectors were being bribed. He thought the bribery was widespread.

To emphasize his point, he told me that the chief workers' compensation fraud investigator in Ontario was a Liberal party appointee who had a prior fraud conviction himself. He ran the show for four years until he was convicted in June 1993 of a criminal offence. Another employee was caught and convicted of embezzling $1 million by fabricating claims from defunct companies and collecting the money himself.

Rings ripped off workers' compensation routinely. There was the Toronto cabbie, for example, who was convicted for fabricating taxi charges which were paid by workers' compensation allegedly for the transport of injured workers. He said many "injured" workers are non-existent, and the only identification — social insurance numbers — are easily counterfeited. One ring of fraudsters — whom I brought to police attention personally — was bringing in illegal labourers from Portugal, obtaining bogus social insurance numbers, and then making fraudulent claims for workers' compensation and unemployment insurance, receiving multiple benefits for years after the workers went home.

One of the worst cases of abuse involved a convicted felon who purposely drove his fork-lift truck while out on bail and feigned a back injury. He was sentenced after the incident to five years' imprisonment, and the gambit relieved him of physical labour while imprisoned and also insured him 90 per cent of his salary for as long as he could fake his back problem.

THE MOTHER OF BOONDOGGLES: UNEMPLOYMENT INSURANCE

Allan MacFarlane was nearly the victim of an unemployment insurance fraud in 1992. He had an employee (a Vietnamese immigrant) who wanted to keep working, but also wanted technically to "quit" then rejoin, using another social insurance number. The reason the employee offered was that she had been working under her unemployed sister's social insurance number. If she quit, then her sister could claim (read: defraud) the unemployment insurance system by claiming benefits because the required period for working had taken place. Then, the worker suggested, she could be "rehired" under her own social insurance number and continue to work.

MacFarlane fired her and reported her to unemployment insurance investigators. He thinks she was stopped from claiming benefits, but she should have gone to jail for fraud. The police were not called in. They never are. A few weeks later, MacFarlane had to fire another employee and was sued for wrongful dismissal. In a letter, his former employee's lawyer wrote cheekily: "We have advised our client that he need not accept even a similar job, if it provides a significantly lesser remuneration. In today's economy, it would take our client a substantial period of time to find a job with similar responsibilities and similar remuneration."

This was another example of Canadians turning unemployment insurance into a slush fund. This time it was for litigants. Similarly a friend was severed permanently from her job, given a few months' pay, but decided to go on unemployment benefits even though, as a systems analyst, she had the pick of jobs or contracts. "I've paid in all these years so I thought I'd take 'my' year off" was her shiftless attitude.

The point is, unemployment insurance has deteriorated from being a scheme to help people while they look for work to become a scheme to help people avoid work. And, like welfare, we're not talking about peanuts. Unemployment insurance has become nearly as costly as Old Age Security payments, and just as badly run as workers' compensation. Government officials have added claimable benefits to vastly outweigh the premiums collected, running up an enormous shortfall despite record-high levies to workers and employers.

Even when there are some curbs on behaviour, they are all too easily circumvented, as the wife of a small entrepreneur pointed out to me in an interview in 1993. She called, distressed at what she perceived to be a scam. Her husband, a carpenter, employed three or four persons at a time, depending upon his workload. He put an advertisement in a daily newspaper and was flooded with phone calls. Weeks later, several more phoned, even though the ad had not run for weeks. They said they wanted details — "so I can put it down on my unemployment insurance form," she was told. "Two out of every three who called said they needed the company name and they purposely picked an old advertisement because they guessed the job would have been filled already. This is abusing the system — to pretend to be looking for work cynically."

In some regions, unemployment insurance looked like it was smartening up a bit. Too bad others did not follow suit.

A British Columbia welfare worker said that, beginning in 1992, unemployment officials circulated a list to welfare offices containing the names and social insurance numbers of unemployment insurance recipients. Unfortunately, only the data for those on unemployment in Vancouver were distributed, a problem since people could easily get benefits from elsewhere in the province or country. But it was a start.

"We had a few cases where the names of welfare recipients appeared on the UIC lists," the worker said. "And you cannot get unemployment insurance unless you have worked. So how could these people have become eligible? They got called in, and in some cases admitted they had been working for years. The result was that they did not have to pay back what they had received over the years. It was categorized as an overpayment. They could still claim assistance, and if [they did] the government would knock off $10 or $15 each month."

I have bumped into UIC beneficiaries drinking beer at Whistler during ski season, on beaches in Mexico, and even in Hungary. How these people can receive assistance when they are supposed to be looking for, and be available for, work is beyond me. A newspaper story in July 1993 said that unemployment insurance claims were made by 642 people living in the United States. It went on to say that interstate claims were more restrictive than standard claims: The average benefit period was "just" thirteen weeks, and a withholding tax of 25 per cent was deducted. Why? No one can say why because nobody knows.

But the greatest abuse occurs in Atlantic Canada, where unemployment insurance is a way of life. In fact, the employers and employees both are geared up to milk it for all it's worth. Because of its high unemployment levels, Atlantic Canada has more generous benefits than elsewhere. Workers needed to work only ten weeks to get forty-two weeks' worth of benefits — the "10–42," as everyone there refers to it. These benefits will be trimmed a bit by the Liberals. But that's not enough. Nearly half of all people working in Newfoundland receive unemployment benefits in any given year. The figures are worse in rural areas, where 70 per cent collect. The population of 600,000 Newfoundlanders are an unsustainable drain, costing their province $220 million, and unemployment insurance $1 billion a year.

In 1993, Newfoundland unveiled a bold reform for social welfare and suggested a guaranteed annual income scheme. Discredited, one hopes, such a plan is terrifying, given the total incompetence of postwar governments involved in virtually any social spending. Goodness help Canada should a gigantic, national plan such as the elusive and foolish "negative income tax" ever come about. That, along with the mountain of abuses outlined above, will finally turn off the lights.

These entitlements account for more than $100 billion of tax dollars per year. Canadians deserve no less than a strict accounting as to where, on whom, and why their money is spent. They deserve new policies. They deserve something for their money. They want reform. For instance, it is only fair that welfare recipients work for their cheques. This would prevent recipients from working illegally or laying about on holiday.

Canada must also carefully screen and limit entrants into our country. For instance, Canada should never accept immigrants from any nation which does not agree to share tax and other private information. Revenue Canada should audit all foreign private schools immediately to find the students' landlords and make sure they are paying taxes on rents. Canada clearly needs to do what France did after it was deluged with illegal aliens giving birth so they could stay with their "French" children. In 1993, it amended its citizenship act; now, those born in France to foreign parents must return home, but can apply for French citizenship when they are eighteen years of age.

Tougher action is needed. In addition to changing citizenship privileges, as the French have done, Canada should require mothers to prove they paid for their children's birth and, if they also defrauded the health system, their children should be denied citizenship and they should be deported. In addition, the offspring of any non-status tourist in Canada should not even qualify for citizenship. Similarly, children born to refugees before scheduled citizenship hearings should not qualify as citizens either. Let families reunite, but have relatives pay the full cost of health, education, and welfare services for at least ten years.

It's important to note here that foreigners are not the only newcomers whose privileges should be stopped. It's also unfair to extend medical benefits to Canadians who left the country for a period of time and did not pay any income taxes.

It's obvious that the provinces must deliver health care in a different way. The Liberals seemed bent on prohibiting extra billing so that a second-tier system — with expensive private care and standard public care — could reduce costs and relieve pressure. But hospitals must close, user fees must be introduced, many procedures must be eliminated from the free list, the number of physicians must be reduced by closing medical schools for a four-year period, and featherbedding by doctors must end. During the late 1980s, there was a 39 per cent increase in the number of doctors, even though population growth during that time was not proportional. New doctors are hungry for fees to survive, so they overservice patients. Many friends talk about having to return more frequently to their doctors for more tests. Probably the reason is they need the income. Doctors also are a trade union which jealously guards certain tasks such as childbirth, physicals, and the like, even though it is proven elsewhere that specialized nurses can do the job for considerably less cost.

Provinces also fail to require doctors to issue patients a duplicate of the charges they are applying for from governments. This would prevent fraud by doctors and also make taxpayers realize how much they are costing themselves. Instead, the door is left wide open for crooked doctors who can pad, or concoct, charges as they wish without anyone checking up on them. I'm told this happens all the time.

To date, Canadian taxpayers have been victimized by a thoroughly inept social spending system. If a bank ran its affairs the way Canadian governments distribute social-program dollars, it would be out of business in no time. Same applies to nations.

THE ENEMIES
OF CANADA

I N THE 1960s, QUEBEC'S SEPARATIST UNDERGROUND SUD-
denly surfaced, blowing up mail boxes and people, and
then turning to kidnapping and murder. The terrorists
were eventually run to ground or to Cuba, but a form of
politicized ruthlessness took their place. The Parti Québécois legitimized the separatist cause by offering its theol-
ogy at the ballot box. And for most of two decades, the
province's separatists have steadily and doggedly mined away
at the country's core. They have also eroded the human rights
of anglophones in Quebec and sparked the biggest migration
in Canadian history since the United Empire Loyalists
descended upon Canada.

Whether Quebeckers want to leave or not is beside the point.
The separatists have infiltrated Quebec's government bureaucracy, media, and academic establishment, and used their
power to manipulate events. Their tactics are despicable.
Equally despicable has been the pandering to Quebec by

Quebec-born prime ministers. Their preoccupation with the unity issue has contributed to the mismanagement of the country and widespread disillusionment among many Canadians.

It's now obvious that the federal strategy has not worked. Not only has separatism now reached the House of Commons itself with the election of 53 Bloc Québécois members of Parliament, but the mishandling of the debt, immigration, and many other policies has given Quebeckers good reason to leave. Like Canadians in general, Quebeckers find their loyalty to Ottawa strained under the burden of taxes.

This reality has played into the hands of the separatists. Canadians have much to be concerned about if they succeed in breaking up the country. Unfortunately, we probably have more to fear if they fail, as separatists are nasty people, and the more violent members of that movement may revert to blowing up mail boxes and the other extreme tactics they employed in the 1960s.

My encounters with Quebec's separatist thought police have been among the most unpleasant I have experienced as a journalist. I wrote a column in *The Financial Post* in November 1991 which stated the obvious: no matter how any sovereignty referendum turned out, Ottawa, and therefore all Canadians, would have the final say over whether, and under what terms, any part of this country left. I wrote that, if Parti Québécois leader Jacques Parizeau and his separatists attempted unilateral secession, without successfully negotiating an exit agreed to by all Canadians, they would be committing treason and should be arrested.

That column caused a stir. I was libelled and pilloried in the Quebec press for stating what merely happens to be the law of the land. Under our constitution, provincial boundary changes can legally be made only by the national Parliament.

The stand-off at Oka in 1991 is a good example of what should happen in cases of insurrection. When the Mohawk "warriors" attempted to seize control of a chunk of Quebec, troops were called in and charges laid. Would-be secessionists should always face such treatment, no matter what language they speak.

One month after my incendiary column was published, I was named *Chatelaine* magazine's "Woman of the Year." And *Chatelaine*'s Montreal offices had to be evacuated because of a bomb threat. The caller who made the threat was upset that a "bigot" such as myself would be given such an honour. Ironically, the caller was apparently unaware that *Chatelaine*'s French-language sister publication had selected its own, different "Woman of the Year." Even so, dozens of subscriptions were cancelled, and some of *The Financial Post*'s vending boxes in Montreal were damaged or defaced, perhaps coincidentally.

It's obvious that Quebec separatists do not believe in freedom of speech. They have shown themselves, in some cases, to be capable of violence, and even murder. But even those who don't resort to physical brutality are intellectual bullies. They don't care what they have to do to achieve their goal, and what they have done has contributed mightily toward the destruction of Canada.

Those within Quebec who dare to oppose the separatist cause are shunned and punished in subtle ways. The Parti Québécois and its followers have succeeded in driving many anglophones from the province while co-opting or frightening those who have remained behind. As for francophones, they have controlled the French-language media and subjected Quebeckers to separatist propaganda for two decades.

The censorship imposed on Quebeckers is widespread and

virulent. I had a weekly column in *Le Soleil* in Quebec City until I wrote that the notion of separatism was, in economic terms, extremely naïve. I indicated that the value of Quebec's exports did not even come close to matching the imports of oil and natural gas it needed to survive. I was promptly relieved of my column in *Le Soleil* and was amused to read, some months later, that some Quebec entity had announced a massive natural-gas discovery in the province. It was so large, according to the report, that Quebec could become a net exporter of the stuff. Needless to say, this was false propaganda designed to counter arguments such as mine that energy dependence tethered Quebec to Canada.

When Quebec's biased media machine isn't lying, it's intimidating its opponents. A month after the *Chatelaine* bomb scare, I was invited by a *Montreal Gazette* reporter to participate in a workshop hosted by the Quebec Journalists' Federation to address the question "Editorial Writers and Columnists. Is Everything Fair Game?"

I knew it would be an ambush so I initially declined. The reporter then challenged me, saying that I couldn't write a column about Parizeau's treason without coming into French Canada to defend it. So I took the bait and flew to Montreal. It seemed to me to be appalling that journalists in a free society would even debate self-censorship, but this was Canada, where oppressive libel and "hate" laws undermined both freedom of speech and democratic rights. Quebec, I was to learn, was even more oppressive.

The workshop, as it turned out, was neither a discussion nor a debate, but a ninety-minute attack on me specifically, and on freedom of speech in general. I was accused of being demagogic and irresponsible. I was insulted. My American background was held against me. And, near the end of this frenzied inquisition, the lowest, and most poorly expressed, blow was delivered by a plump public relations woman who informed me that I "struck a chord of shit" with English Canada.

These were not low-level *paparazzi* but prominent journalists. And yet they were utterly intolerant of contrary opinions, and favoured censorship when it suited them. They actually thought that I did not have the right to state the obvious in a column to my readers about a public issue of national importance. The French-Canadian moderator was no less rabid than the French-Canadian journalists in the audience, while those in the English-language press remained silent. But Quebec's English press are timid souls for the most part, and made more timid by displays against me and others.

A few days before this shabby treatment at the hands of fellow journalists, commentator Laurier La Pierre scolded French Canada's press for censoring facts to further separatist causes. He too was attacked. So was McGill University professor Stephen Scott for agreeing with me that Quebec could not legally secede without the Parliament of Canada's approval. His academic colleagues actually responded by asking him, and others, to sign a petition saying that his opinions were not shared by everyone, and that they did not represent the views of McGill University. This was a disgraceful, and cowardly, example of people who are entitled to academic freedom distancing themselves from a colleague who practised it.

TWO SOLITUDES

Canada has always been two "nations." But the two have grown farther apart for a variety of reasons. English Canada is becoming increasingly American, while Quebec's development has been shaped by an élite of separatists who are every bit as narrow, rigid, and undemocratic as was the Roman Catholic clergy who ran their forebears' lives for centuries. For three decades, separatists have schemed and plotted to bring about the independence of the province. After the defeat of the FLQ and the failure of the Parti Québécois, Quebec nationalists set out to achieve by discriminatory legislation an ethnic cleansing of the province. This led to the exodus over twenty years of an estimated 400,000 anglophones and hundreds of corporate head offices.

The separatist notion that a unique, francophone state can be created swims against the current. French, like Welsh, is a doomed language. A few people may always speak it, but, within a generation, the world will mostly speak English, Mandarin, and Spanish. Quebec is situated in a hemisphere dominated by people who speak English, Spanish, and (in Brazil) Portuguese. Only Haitians share the French tongue. Like it or not, in order to survive within Canada or within the North American free-trade area, Quebeckers must know English, Spanish, and (possibly) Portuguese.

Undaunted by such unwelcome realities, Quebec leaders have created their tiny corporatist state headed by Hydro-Québec, the Caisse de dépot et placement du Québec, and a host of crown corporations and a few favoured francophone private-sector proxies. Many crown corporations were created by the supposedly federalist governments formed by the Quebec Liberal party, but the underlying objective was to build the foundation either for more independence or for outright separation.

During the 1970s, the acrimony between Ottawa and Quebec City culminated in two critically important events: the referendum of 1980 and the debate over the constitution and

Charter of Rights and Freedoms in 1982. The referendum was soundly defeated, but it represented a huge strategic victory for sovereigntists. By acceding to a plebiscite, the federal government implicitly accepted the concept of self-determination by a minority. This somewhat undermines the argument that only Parliament can give permission for a change of national boundaries.

Stephen Scott wrote that "Quebec cannot secede unilaterally. Canada is a sovereign state, every part of which belongs to all of its people, so far as political sovereignty is concerned. Only through the mechanisms provided by the constitution itself can its territory or its institutions be lawfully altered. Change by any other means is the revolutionary overthrow of the state. There are the two options. There are no others."

Still, even after losing the referendum, the separatists set about to sabotage the 1982 constitution. They did not sign the document, nor did they ever intend to sign it. This led to another decade of acrimonious and damaging constitutional talks, culminating in, first, the Meech Lake and, then, the Charlottetown accords. Canada has been in the midst of a unity crisis for more than a generation.

The crisis has nothing to do with language but everything to do with a power grab by radicals leading a relatively homogeneous, compliant minority. Canadians have accepted federal bilingualism, learned French outside Quebec's borders in record numbers, and accepted Quebec unilingualism. Parizeau, whose party has denied publicly funded English-language education to the children of francophones and immigrants, once admitted to me that every ambitious Quebecker, whether an engineer, academic, researcher, businessman, or politician, had to speak English to get ahead in the world. "Yes," he said, "and I'd like them to speak a third language, too."

Parizeau's cynical use of the language issue and other strategies has contributed to Quebec fatigue — precisely the desired result of a well-honed tactic deployed by Parizeau and others. He described the tactic to me in an interview in late 1990. "All this talk about the constitution and clause this and clause that is tedious. You cannot have a nation based on clauses and sections and paragraphs. French Canadians and English Canadians are sick and tired of it, and yet the politicians will continue to talk for years about clauses and sections and paragraphs until everybody gets fed up and says enough is enough," he said.

So, by stirring up the constitutional debate whenever possible, Parizeau and his separatists have steadily worn thin English Canada's patience and divided the country. They also helped elect Brian Mulroney as prime minister, and this paid handsome dividends. Mulroney was totally preoccupied with Quebec issues — as was Trudeau — and undeniably biased in favour of the nationalists.

During Mulroney's term in office, the Supreme Court of Canada struck down as unconstitutional Quebec's restrictive sign by-law which forbade the use of English, even in English stores. The court found that the law contravened the freedom-of-expression rights under the Charter of Rights and Freedoms. Unfortunately, the constitution also permitted provinces to opt out of certain charter decisions for five years at a time. Quebec opted out, and the sign by-law continued in force. That provoked furious opposition in English Canada, where the trend was toward placing more emphasis on individual, rather than group, rights. Mulroney could have overridden the opt-out as prime minister and forced Quebec to remove the sign by-law, but chose not to.

Quebec writer Mordecai Richler wrote a series of essays,

published as *Oh, Canada Oh, Quebec,* which described the "tongue troops" and other apparatchiks who prowled the streets and prosecuted people for signs in English. When excerpts appeared in *The New Yorker* magazine, the Quebec government was embarrassed. Pressure was also exerted on the Quebec government as a result of a ruling by a United Nations committee which indicated that the sign by-law contravened international human-rights provisions Canada had agreed to uphold.

No action was ever taken against the by-law by Mulroney's appointee — former NDP leader Ed Broadbent — who headed the International Centre for Human Rights and Democratic Development in Montreal. Broadbent said that, while Quebec infringed the human rights of its anglophone minority, this was an "acceptable trade-off" to preserve collective rights of the francophone majority. "Sometimes there is a minor infraction of one right for the community right of the majority, and I've accepted that," he said.

At a public meeting held into the issue in March 1994 with Broadbent, a Montreal woman shouted: "We are not minorities. We are not anglophones. We are Canadians."

Fortunately, by 1994, the sign by-law was virtually gutted, but no thanks to Parliament or the constitution.

With Mulroney's unwitting complicity, the Parti Québécois made hay during the 1980s, even as mere opposition. Perhaps Mulroney's biggest mistake was the attempt to co-opt charismatic separatists Lucien Bouchard, Marcel Masse, and Gilles Loiselle by giving them important cabinet posts. "Mulroney brought into the very heart of Canada many of the extreme nationalists committed to the development of a sovereign Quebec and gave control of key ministries to Lucien Bouchard, Marcel Masse, and Gilles Loiselle," wrote Quebec politician Maurice King in his book *The First Step*, published in November 1993.

Bouchard even got from Mulroney the ultimate patronage plum for a Quebecker, the ambassadorship to France. This job gave Bouchard insight and prestige that he could have obtained in no other way. After Bouchard resigned in disgust over the failure of Meech Lake, he was propelled into the separatist big leagues and launched, with other Quebec Tories and Liberals, his own separatist party at the federal level. In the federal election in 1993, he parlayed his popularity into a massive sweep of the province and became opposition leader. From this eminent situation he functioned as though he were External Affairs minister for the Republic of Quebec. In 1994 he went to see United Nations secretary general Boutros Boutros-Ghali in New York City and U.S. government officials in Washington. This was a cunning manoeuvre designed to convince the world and American leaders that the separation of Quebec will not be an outlaw act, even if opposed by English Canada. Instead, he put forward the view that independence is the next step in the necessary self-determination of a minority through democratic means.

Here's how Bouchard rationalized the justification for unilateral secession in a speech he gave March 1994 in Washington, D.C.: "This will be a democratic decision made by the people of Quebec in a peaceful and quite adequate way. And then the Canadian government and all governments in the world will have to take into account the fact that democracy has expressed itself in Quebec and that it has to be accepted as a fact."

When asked if this amounted to the breaking up of a viable state, he responded, "No, we are not breaking a state because the state of Canada did not pre-exist the state of Quebec. We entered into a federation in 1867. We have accepted a deal, and the deal has been broken in 1982 by the federal government who ganged up with the English-speaking provinces of Canada to impose a constitution on Quebec that was a breach of faith. We are a nation. We feel like a nation. We have a territory. We have a most viable economy and as long as we respect the democratic rules the United Nations has a resolution which allows us to get out of the federation."

McGill professor Stephen Scott argues that that's not true and, if Canada is divisible for reasons of self-determination, then so is what's now known as Quebec. "To Parizeau and Bouchard no one but the majority of Quebec's electors has any rights of self-determination at all. Native peoples who have surrendered aboriginal rights of property are said to have surrendered also their claims to leave or to self-determination. Natives who have retained aboriginal rights are, however, said to possess nothing more than property rights. International law is invoked as supporting all of his positions. It is one great tissue of hypocrisy, dishonesty and deception."

CHEATING THE NEIGHBOURS

Through a host of protectionist laws, Quebec has treated its confederation partners badly. Non-tariff barriers obstruct trade between Quebec and other provinces, and yet Ottawa has been helpless for years to negotiate their removal.

In the absence of fair trading rules, businessmen from outside Quebec have been routinely harassed and impeded when they try to work within the province in contravention of both the Free Trade Agreement and General Agreement on Tariffs and Trade. The Atlantic provinces have been little better, routinely imposing a 5 per cent "tariff" on goods and services from outside the region. But Quebec has been the worst culprit, by far. It has not only subsidized "exports" to the rest of Canada but restricts tendering inside Quebec.

For years, bids were invited in Quebec in the *Daily Commercial News*, but the ads usually stated that "only those having their principal place of business in Quebec can bid." This meant that non-Quebeckers, like Ontario stainless-steel fabricator Hercules Food Equipment Limited, were being underbid in their own province by Quebec fabricators who were indirectly subsidized by their provincial government. Hercules and others approached me after they failed to interest Ontario's government in going to bat for them against Quebec's unfair trade restrictions. They had collectively lost almost every major contract in Ontario to two Quebec-based rivals who were subsidized by their provincial government and protected from competition in Quebec.

"The Quebec-based companies are virtually stealing jobs from us. The province of Quebec is playing an unfair game. They are making all the rules, while the rest of Canada sits back and watches," wrote Paul Cesario, president of Trimen Food Service Equipment Inc. in Toronto, another steel fabricator.

"Quebec cheats and subsidizes," said Trimen partner Suzan Stilling. To prove her point, she talked with officials from Quebec's Société de Développement in 1991 about relocating her operation to Quebec. She said they gave her propaganda and a sales pitch about all the subsidies she could receive if she moved.

"I wanted to find out how much they subsidized, and I was absolutely disgusted," she said. "Two Quebec representatives [from Société de Développement] sat in our office for about two hours. They gave me literature and cannot deny what's in it. I asked about exports, and the representatives defined exports as 'anything outside Quebec.'"

Others have come forward with similar stories over the years. G.D. Finnen, president of Golden Windows Ltd. in Kitchener, Ontario, for example, said that wood-window manufacturers from Quebec have also been subsidized for years by Quebec to steal market share in Ontario. For public-policy purposes, Quebec City has regarded the rest of Canada as a foreign country.

For years, Quebec construction workers escaping union restrictions inside their own province flooded into Ontario (especially Ottawa) and New Brunswick. Meanwhile, workers from other provinces were not allowed to work in Quebec because of Quebec's protectionist work-permit system.

Another case of Quebec protectionism was that of Harry Bligh of Ottawa. Bligh, a member of the glass and aluminium workers' union, said he and Ontario workers are denied the right to work in Quebec. "I cannot work in Quebec without a permit unless I get 6,000 hours work from a Quebec company, and I can't get 6,000 hours work from a Quebec company without a permit. And our government in Ontario is too stupid to do anything about this."

Worse, he said, "we can't deliver windows on the Quebec side if we don't have trucks with Quebec plates. The Quebec police are involved and pull over Ontario-licensed commercial vehicles for any excuse. Meanwhile, Quebec trucks are delivering Quebec stuff over here all the time."

The rules require that working materials and labour must be from Quebec, he says. "Remember the museum in Hull with Ontario material that had to be torn up. Hundreds of thousands of tax dollars went down the drain because of that," he says.

Stones had been laid around the Museum of Civilization, but because they were not from Quebec they were ripped up and replaced with local stone at great expense. This was an outrageous example of favouritism, particularly since the museum was a federal project paid for by all Canadian taxpayers.

Another example of Quebec's cheating involved Cancoppas Ltd., a high-tech, environmental-control equipment company in Toronto run by John Coomey. A member of the Ontario Pollution Control Equipment Association, he and his rivals have tried to stop Quebec's discriminatory tender-bid requirements forbidding manufacturers like them from bidding on Quebec public-sector contracts. But even more insulting, Coomey had a run-in with Quebec officials in 1993 when he sent his staff in a rented truck to a pulp and paper trade show in Montreal. The truck contained the booth and other display equipment that the company needed to show off its wares at the trade show.

"One mile from the Ontario border, coming back, our truck was stopped by the Quebec department of transport police. Our driver was fined $371 for not having a permit to drive the truck into Quebec, plus he had to buy the $112 permit, for a total of $483. On top of all that, he had to pay in cash, and the police drove him to a bank right there and then. He used his credit card to get the money, paid the fine, and since then we've had a notice to appear in court in Valleyfield on charges that we drove without a permit in Quebec. We sent it back and said we're not going to court. It's finished now."

The permit requirements are clearly in place to discourage businesses from bringing their trucks into Quebec from outside the province. The cargo in this truck was for business use. Coomey was displaying his products and spending money at a convention in Quebec. As thanks, he got hit with fines, aggravation, and insults. If the driver hadn't had a bank card, he would have been put in jail. Imagine one Canadian province putting a Canadian citizen in jail for driving his car on highways he helped to pay for!

"I'm continually upset with Quebec," said Coomey. "We drive our trucks to Vancouver and back and never get stopped."

In May 1994, Ontario and Quebec announced with great fanfare a bilateral "free trade" deal which would remove labour and tendering restrictions. Long overdue, the deal was greeted with scepticism. Some of us will have to see Quebec treat its neighbours fairly before we believe it.

QUEBEC'S CORPORATISM FIASCO

Separatists have seized large chunks of Quebec's economy for various political ends. Economic monoliths, such as Hydro-Québec, are levers to be pulled in order to facilitate independence, reduce dependence upon the rest of Canada, punish economic dissidents within the province, reward political colleagues within the province, and ruthlessly lessen competition from outsiders.

Whatever the motivation and purpose, the nationalistic "corporatist" experiment has failed for the most part, according to Pierre Arbour, who was a ranking member of the Quebec establishment. Arbour wrote a controversial book in 1993 called *Quebec Inc. and the Temptation of State Capitalism* which debunks the myth that state capitalism or linguistic restrictions in Quebec have benefited francophones.

Arbour's criticism caused the usual stir among separatist

apologists. He drew fire particularly because he is a franco-phone who worked from 1967 to 1979 as a portfolio manager at Quebec's pension giant, the Caisse de dépot et placement du Québec, in Montreal. As Arbour documents in his book, Quebec has had the country's most interventionist, and mis-guided, government. But it's hardly alone.

"The temptation of state intervention is a temptation every government has had," Arbour said to me in an interview in his Montreal office in fall 1993. For instance, he said, there was the Alberta government's involvement with Novatel Commu-nications Ltd.; British Columbia's British Columbia Resources Investment Corp.; the federal government with Petro-Canada and scores of other money-losing crown corporations; Ontario with the Urban Transportation Development Corp.

As for Quebec, he wrote: "the real losers are not the rich, not the anonymous private investors in the market, but the whole population of Quebec, passive and captive to events decided without their approval. All Quebeckers, as unwilling shareholders, emerged poorer from these adventures."

In his book, Arbour takes on the Caisse and other "sacred cows" in Quebec and deals with another taboo: "I give my reflections on another kind of state intervention, the linguistic laws whose constraining clutch is, together with high taxa-tion, partially responsible for the relative impoverishment of Quebec at a time when we are at a critical stage of our devel-opment as a francophone community."

Arbour is now a successful entrepreneur, involved in a number of venture-capital projects such as oil and gas limited partnerships in Western Canada; the privatization of Tijuana Airport in Mexico; and financing for cable television systems. He took the time off to write his book because of his concern about governments and the mishandling of funds.

He believes that the Caisse, which manages the $15-billion Quebec Pension Plan, plus billions more in pension and mandatory provincial automobile insurance funds, has not made the return that it could have made. "The Caisse is supposed to have made 11.7 per cent return. That's their figure. But I believe it could have made 1 per cent more."

While 11.7 per cent is respectable, Arbour's point is that another one percentage point of return is another 8 per cent higher return. Besides that, the Caisse has justified its Draconian and sweeping mandate by maintaining that these strategies ensure the highest possible returns. No matter which way the Caisse and other provincial economic instruments are described, they are merely a Quebec version of interventionist, socialist statism.

Arbour showed that most of what Parizeau initiated, and the Liberals kept, has been a flop. About the only successes are government-owned monopolies Gaz Métropolitain and Hydro-Québec. Some would say that Hydro-Québec has been far from successful, that, in fact, it is bloated and overexposed to debt, and has indulged in questionable accounting games.

Arbour estimates the Quebec Stock Savings Plan scheme cost Quebec's treasury $1 billion from 1979 to 1985. High rollers could write off 100 per cent of their investments in new Quebec companies and 25 per cent in existing ones. "The big winners were the accountants, lawyers, and brokers — not the public," he said.

Other basket cases include Sidbec, Dosco, Asbestos Corp., Quebecair, Petromont, and Davies Shipbuilding (a shipyard which he described as a "living nightmare"). Arbour said the Steinberg Inc. saga cost the Caisse $448 million in losses because it would not allow the grocery-store chain to be sold to an Ontario outfit which bid that much more. The Brascade-

Noranda Mines Ltd. losses he estimated were $858 million, and Domtar cost Quebeckers $117 million plus lost interest. Then there are the unknown costs resulting from unfair linguistic policies and high taxation rates to pay for state interventions. As Arbour said, unfair language laws cost Montreal its pre-eminence as Canada's head-office capital, and the exodus cost Quebec an estimated $1 billion a year in lost taxes.

"It is still possible for Quebec to act," said Arbour, "by making a fundamental change in its language laws to make them compatible with the Charter of Rights and Freedoms and to modify its tax levels to allow us to be more competitive, to become a more attractive place to transact business than we have recently been — compared to our Canadian, American and Mexican neighbours."

THE LOOMING BACKLASH

The unending federal pandering to Quebec demands has been aided and abetted by the Ottawa élite, which, after two decades of bilingualization, is now pretty much dominated by francophones. The Prime Minister's Office has been run by Quebec-born politicians. The result is that Canada's perpetual unity crisis is really a struggle between Ottawa's federalist francophones and Quebec's separatist francophones. The rest of the country has been caught in the crossfire.

The rise of the Reform Party is a symptom of a profound shift in attitude against these élites and toward a responsive, American-style democracy. Historian Michael Bliss of the University of Toronto agrees. "We didn't join the U.S. because we didn't like democracy. But now we have too much élite government — all these constitutional wrangles are about boys making deals, macho games, élites using power to give themselves a comfortable life. Business used governments to protect themselves from becoming competitive against the Americans. Now labour unions do. Even Canada's judiciary is trying to figure out democracy and has trouble letting the press into court cases.

"I opposed the charter because I thought it would Americanize Canada," Bliss continued. "I was wrong. Since then I've come to see we must follow the democratic path the Americans have blazed. California [with its voter referendums] is the future, and now we are starting to bring human rights into our democracy through the charter. This is the age of blossoming individualism. The U.S. has always been the beacon of liberty to the world, and Canada is trying to catch up."

Unfortunately, Ottawa's élite controls the purse strings, and the nation's debts are, in great measure, the result of the damaging preoccupation with Quebec among Ottawa's ministers and mandarins. Quebec gamesmanship has virtually paralysed the federal government, preventing it from undertaking even the most preliminary, painful reforms for fear of alienating the province. Instead, Parliament has doled out favours, grants, equalization payments, and transfers to keep the peace.

The worst example of favouritism may have destroyed the Tory party for years to come. In the mid-1980s, a $1-billion maintenance contract for the CF-18 jet was won fair and square by tender bidding by a British-owned aerospace company in Winnipeg. After intense lobbying and an appeal to the federal cabinet by Quebeckers, Mulroney's government totally abandoned the tendering process and awarded the contract to Canadair Inc. in Montreal. It was a flagrant and damaging example of Quebec pork-barrelling and, not coincidentally, months later the Reform Party was launched in the West.

Other annoying examples of the federal bias in favour of Quebec interests include: Marcel Masse's attempt while Defence minister to transfer most of the armed forces offices and equipment out of Ontario and into Quebec; the acceptance by Ottawa of separate status for Quebec in the commonwealth of francophone nations; and the establishment in St. Hubert, Quebec, of the $80.5-billion Canadian Space Agency, billed as "an agency which might be the best way to keep the country together," and which now answers the phone only in French and has dropped the word "Canadian" from its title.

The Office of the Commission of Official Languages cost Canadians $655.9 million in 1993–94, up from $504 million in 1986–87. By 1991–92, the Official Languages Act had facilitated the domination of francophones in Ottawa. In the general population, Canada comprises 73.4 per cent anglophones and 25.2 per cent francophones. But a sampling shows how skewed in favour of francophones the federal government has become. The Canadian Radio-television and Telecommunications Commission (CRTC) is 51.4 per cent anglophone and 48.6 per cent francophone. The competitions tribunal is only 25 per cent anglophone and 75 per cent francophone. Elections Canada is 21 per cent anglophone and 79 per cent francophone. The Official Languages Office is 27.7 per cent anglophone and 72.3 per cent francophone. The Secretary of State is 22.9 per cent anglophone and 77.1 per cent francophone. The CBC is 55.6 per cent anglophone and 44.4 per cent francophone. The Canada Council is 48.5 per cent anglophone and 51.5 per cent francophone.

In the early days of Prime Minister Jean Chrétien's regime there were signs of more pandering to Quebec. His government's first budget, in February 1994, failed to make any deep spending cuts, probably out of concern that tough and unpopular action would enhance the Parti Québécois's chances of beating the Liberals in the next Quebec provincial election.

That budget also showed how skilful the separatist propagandists can be at escalating an insignificant spending-cut issue into a matter of provincial pride. Chrétien's budget announced that the Royal Military College in Quebec would be permanently closed to save costs. Despite the disdain for the word "Royal," much less the fact that Quebec has never adequately supported Canada's defence or its military, Bouchard was able to make political hay over the closure.

Chrétien's government again caved in to Quebec, in April 1994, when it cancelled a preliminary discussion with Quebec and the other provinces about social-spending reforms. Then Quebec premier Daniel Johnson threatened to boycott the meeting and demanded that Ottawa transfer to his province all federal responsibility for manpower training, a key component of the social program changes. He then accused the federal government of attempting to unilaterally impose its vision on social programs. To cap it all, Johnson's Liberals then backed a separatist party motion unanimously supporting Quebec's right to exercise exclusive jurisdiction over manpower training. It was a case of a simple meeting being escalated by the separatist machine into an issue of independence.

Canada's current fiscal crisis can be traced to the fact that federal cabinets since Pierre Elliott Trudeau's initial election have been the political version of a board of directors more preoccupied with revamping the corporation's by-laws, or with pleasing certain shareholders, than with drumming up new business or with improving operations. The fall 1993 election exposed the fault lines and the vulnerability of the nation itself. So did the initial actions taken by the Liberals.

The February 1994 budget was a Quebec-driven disaster, and then, in March 1994, Prime Minister Chrétien underscored the destructive mentality by appointing a francophone constitutional expert to be in charge of his office. It looked like Ottawa would be preoccupied with Quebec for the rest of the decade.

Ironically, the Quebec problem has harmed Quebec more than any other issue in Canada. As the province's economic condition deteriorates, the rest of the country is dragged down with it. Quebec, for instance, loses economic activity as a result of its linguistic and economic policies. Its share of the GDP has dropped from 24 to 21 per cent since the early 1970s; its unemployment has remained consistently higher than the national average, or 14 per cent in 1993 compared with 11 per cent; and its portion of federal debt plus its soaring provincial debt are equivalent to 122 per cent of its entire economic output, second only to Newfoundland, whose debts are 160 per cent of its GDP. Even worse, interest payments on Quebec's debts in 1993 were equivalent to 353.6 per cent of all its exports, compared with Alberta's 106.9 per cent or Ontario's 184.6 per cent. An independent Quebec would sink like a stone under the weight of debts. It would be Slovakia to English Canada's Czech Republic, a smallish entity with considerably diminished prospects.

"Quebec is more dependent on trade with the rest of Canada than the rest of Canada is with Quebec. Some 26.5 per cent of Quebec's manufacturers' shipments went to the rest of Canada in 1984 compared to only 6.8 per cent of the rest of Canada's shipments to Quebec," wrote Patrick Grady in his book *Quebec Gun to Our Heads: The Economic Consequences of Separation.*

Quebec's most important industries face huge problems.

Its largest, paper and allied products, is threatened by environmental concerns and regulations. Its protected sectors, like textiles, clothing, dairy, and furniture, will struggle. It will lose access to oil and natural gas, and will be faced with higher borrowing costs. Hydro-Québec, its last hope, has been losing out as a result of environmental concerns among U.S. users. The Cree and Newfoundland may cut off power to an independent Quebec. Hydro-Québec would also have to end industrial power subsidies before being allowed to join NAFTA. Right now, its subsidies are not covered because Quebec is not a federal government, and the agreement binds only federal jurisdictions.

In the medium to long run, English Canada is better off without Quebec. But whether Quebec leaves or stays, its deteriorating condition and nationalist politics will continue to have an adverse effect on Canada's overall prosperity. "The free trade agreement would probably be about as far as Canada would want to go to accommodate Quebec," wrote Grady. "It would not be an act of magnanimity. It would be in Canada's interests."

But months of hard feelings and haggling over the division of debts and assets will annoy, and probably unite, English Canada. It will also bring about a collapse of Ottawa and Hull real estate values unless Parizeau hires the 25,000 federal civil servants who live in Quebec (which he has promised to do). English Canada, for its part, will dismantle bilingualism and have to cope with the deluge of anglophone, allophone, and possibly francophone loyalists who would prefer to remain Canadians. At the end of the day, concluded Grady, "there would be dire consequences for both."

Equality Party chief Keith Henderson feels that there could be violence in light of the fact that many Quebeckers would refuse to leave or live in an independent republic. "There will be forced violence. What do people do who are suddenly ordered not to remit taxes to Ottawa but to Quebec City? How do you require law-abiding Quebec citizens to break the law? Send in the police? Canada must not abandon law-abiding citizens in Quebec, and a unilateral declaration of independence must be considered an illegal act. Only Parliament can allow Quebec to leave."

Another problem would be Quebec's current boundaries. If Canada is divisible, so is Quebec: the northern two-thirds belong to the Cree, and pockets in and around Montreal and along the Ottawa River would be claimed by anglophones, said Equality Party MLA Neil Cameron from Montreal. Similarly, if a majority of francophones opt for self-determining sovereignty, Cree and anglophones can presumably do the same.

Economics and rational discussion are not the basis of most nation-states. Even so, it amazes me that a separatist leader like Parizeau, for all his credentials as an economist, doesn't care about the damage he and his policies have wreaked upon Quebec over the years. Hundreds of head offices have left and are still departing. After the Bloc swept the province in fall 1993, two transnational firms from France — Alcatel and Liquid Air — quietly moved their North American head offices from Montreal to Toronto. They were undoubtedly concerned about the risk of being suddenly caught in a tiny, unviable independent country.

Similarly, the shutdown until 1996 of an auto plant in Bromont, Quebec, is nothing more than the case of a cautious foreign investor waiting to see whether separation will occur before adding to its investment. The facts are that an independent Quebec would have an economy about the size of Austria's; the highest debts of any industrialized country in the world; and economic prospects equivalent to those of Greece, or worse.

Another Quebec problem is that immigrants have avoided the province because they are denied the right, under Quebec law, to have their taxes go toward the education of their children in the English language. Immigrant parents are entitled to public education for their children only in French. For this reason and others, my husband and I, both born outside Canada, would never have considered living in Quebec when our children were growing up. We would not want our children to be handcuffed to a language diminishing in importance or an economy deteriorating as it is in Quebec. A unilingual Quebec will have a tough time going it alone because of language isolation and because of the hard feelings, and economic problems, it will face. Ironically, in the long run, English Canada is better off financially and politically without Quebec, especially if the split results in greater unity of purpose among English-speaking Canadians.

UNIONS AGAINST WORKERS

SOME 4 MILLION OF CANADA'S 12.3 MILLION workers are forced to pay "taxes" of between $50 and $300 a month in the form of union dues to trade labour-union leaders in Canada and the United States. They must pay whether or not they want to, whether or not they are union members, whether or not they agree with their unions' politics, and whether or not the union earns its dues. Worse yet, these workers have no choice but to pay dues unless they have the huge financial resources necessary to embark on an expensive and difficult decertification process.

Most of Canada's unionized workers never have a choice in the first place. Probably 95 per cent of Canada's 4 million unionized workers were never given a secret ballot so they could make up their own minds about the union that represents them. In the absence of the right to choose what to join and what to not join, one in three Canadians is shackled to a union.

Unions have rarely, if ever, won the consent of those they govern.

Since the Second World War, Canada's governments have abandoned individual rights and, by so doing, allowed the country to become largely a "closed shop" nation. This has condemned many Canadians to unemployment, both directly and indirectly, because artificially high union wages represent an enormous competitive disadvantage. Entire industries are "closed shops" in Canada, from nursing and teaching to public-sector services, the construction trades, mining, forestry, steel, and the auto sector. Shoring up this system are provincial labour laws which are exempted from Canada's meagre constitutional protections.

Canada's entire public sector has gradually been unionized without worker consent since the end of the war. "Thou shalt unionize" was the rule imposed by legislatures responding to repeated requests by union organizers. Now virtually 100 per cent of public-sector employees pay very high union dues without any choice.

But the biggest impediment to freedom and efficiency in the workplace in Canada is the Rand Formula. Judge Ivan Rand rendered the landmark decision in 1946, according to which workers in union shops do not have to "join" a union, but must let that union bargain on their behalf. In return for its bargaining services, the workers must support the union through regular dues deducted from their wages. This was a compromise designed to saw off individual rights and union rights. What the misguided Rand Formula does instead is subordinate individual rights to union rights.

Rand confers on unions the right to tax, a power that, not surprisingly, has given union leaders enormous leverage over the country's political process. In 1989 about $800 million in dues flowed into union coffers from workers who had little or no say as to how their dues money was spent. Through their partnership with the New Democrats, the unions have imposed their agenda onto governments, obtaining strike powers which override private property rights and monopoly powers which run roughshod over individual freedoms.

By 1991, around 32 per cent of Canada's entire workforce was unionized, compared with only 16 per cent in the United States. In fact, Canada's private sector is about as unionized as America's. The significant difference between the two countries is that much of America's public sector is non-union, while Canada's proportionally larger public sector is totally unionized.

One of the most outrageous abuses of union power occurred in 1992 in British Columbia when the province paid 880 striking coal miners at Fording Coal Ltd. in Elkford welfare out of tax dollars to supplement strike pay. This was the first time that taxpayers across Canada subsidized the United Steelworkers of America.

Welfare was designed to support unemployed people. The striking workers were not unemployed. They had well-paying jobs (averaging $50,000 a year) but were refusing to work. As in any disagreement, both sides in this dispute were probably to blame. But, in such a case, both sides should bear the cost of their judgment or actions. They were poles apart after months on strike, and a mediator gave up on the matter and issued a report. The strike eventually ended in late 1992.

The welfare payments were obtained under a special "hardship" provision. In this case, seven months of impasse and meagre strike pay were deemed to constitute hardship. No doubt some union members were against the wall financially. There were defaults on mortgages and impending foreclosures. So when the local town council petitioned the province for help, the province came across with tax dollars.

But a terrible precedent was set. According to a provincial spokesman, "under hardship provisions for persons involved in industrial disputes, there must be written confirmation from the union that workers cannot make ends meet." Naturally, the steelworkers' union obliged with written confirmation.

It could be argued that, by providing welfare for the most vulnerable workers, the province prolonged the strike, and by doing so increased the cost to the majority of workers who did not qualify for "hardship" help. There was also the fact that the union was one of the richest in North America. Why should taxpayers be forced to subsidize one of the richest and most powerful unions on the continent. The union — not taxpayers — should have come up with financial aid for its workers.

Besides exercising such influence over political policy, unions also have enormous leverage over the country's judiciary because they can hire the best and brightest lawyers in the land. A famous illustration of this power occurred in 1982, when an Ontario community college teacher named Merv Lavigne launched a charter challenge intended to win him the right to direct that portion of his union dues to the political party of his choice. Union leaders have complete discretion in disposing of union funds and always chose to support the New Democratic Party. Lavigne, with financial backing of the National Citizens' Coalition, did not want part of his dues to go to the New Democrats because he did not agree with their platform or basic beliefs. It took eight years for his case to wind its way through the Canadian court system to the Supreme Court of Canada. In court nearly one dozen union lawyers faced Lavigne's single counsel. Not surprisingly, the court ruled against Lavigne on the basis that, under freedom-of-assembly provisions, his rights had not been transgressed.

Another case combines union and government oppression. Norma Janzen, a British Columbia teacher of disabled children, was fired in 1990 because she refused to join a union. She had been a teacher since 1969, but, in June 1990, her local school board and a union negotiated a closed-shop provision. She refused to join either the union or the British Columbia Teachers' Federation. The result of this exercise of individual choice was that she lost the means of making a living. Her reason for acting as she did was simple and based on an overriding concern for her disabled pupils.

"I entered this profession because I wanted to help young people, and joining the union would have interfered with that goal," she said. "I had to stand by that principle, even if it meant losing my job. Someone has to stand up for what's right. These laws that infringe on my freedom of association are just plain wrong."

Fortunately, the National Citizens' Coalition took on her case and undertook to pay her legal costs after it was contacted by a group of sympathetic teachers called B.C. Teachers for Association. Like Janzen, many of them refused and unsuccessfully appealed their cases to the Industrial Relations Council. Janzen's lawyer will argue that closed shops violate an individual's freedom of association, guaranteed by section 2(d) of the charter. Janzen is also seeking damages from the school board. If she wins, the others can collect too.

Unfortunately, another of her colleagues, B.C. teacher Hans Rupprecht, has had no legal recourse for years. He also lost his job, and his subsequent personal hardship underscores how ordinary citizens are not protected properly against abuse of their rights in Canada.

Rupprecht argued that his termination also transgressed his

rights. In his case, the rights in question were the freedom to act on the religious beliefs of his choice. He refused the join the union because the British Columbia Teachers' Federation supports abortion on demand and he does not. "In the fall of 1989, I applied for religious exemption from union membership; specifically the requirement to join the Langley Teachers' Association and the federation," he said. His application was denied by the Industrial Relations Council, and he was fired. There is no appeal to decisions made by this council or labour boards in all the provinces.

He decided to take the political route and took his case to the B.C. Council of Human Rights on the basis of section 2(b) of the charter — freedom of thought, belief, opinion, and expression. He argued that his right to practise his religious beliefs was denied because he was being forced to support financially and belong to a group that stood for policies that were contrary to his beliefs. No right-thinking person would deny that was the case. "To date, I have had no response from any labour tribunal, human rights commission, MLA or MP," he said.

I tried to interest the so-called Canadian Civil Liberties Association, but its director, Alan Borovoy, refused to return my faxes or calls for months. Finally, when we were both appearing in a television program and I had the opportunity to talk to him personally, he told me that Rupprecht's problem is not a civil-liberties matter. I disagreed. But there's another angle to this. Borovoy's Civil Liberties Association is supported financially in large measure by trade labour-union leaders, and their representatives sit on his board. Borovoy himself was counsel with the Canadian Labour Congress before creating the association. This is why he, and his board, have never had any appetite for individual rights when they challenge union rights.

Unions have too many rights, and workers too few. Unions also have the power of the purse, thanks to governments which force those same workers to contribute to union coffers. The problem is that no individual alone can take on the unions in this country. This is the case even if the union's actions are clearly unconstitutional. It's just too expensive. A charter challenge can cost $500,000 in legal fees and take years if it goes all the way to the Supreme Court. The National Citizens' Coalition took on Janzen's case in the hope that it would set an important precedent for all workers who have been forced to join unions against their will.

"It is terrible that someone has to spend that amount of money to protect their rights from a government which doesn't give a damn," said National Citizens' Coalition head David Somerville.

Unfortunately, shortly after her case was launched, the wealthy Canadian Labour Congress embarked on a cunning new strategy which, if successful, would further violate her rights and those of all Canadians seeking redress under the Charter of Rights. The congress asked the B.C. Supreme Court for "intervenor status" in her case. This was fine, but, for the first time in Canadian jurisprudence, the court, and a subsequent appeal court, ruled that the congress could not only intervene but also recoup its full legal costs from Janzen if she lost her case. This was extraordinary, considering that the congress could not be considered an injured party.

These decisions have huge implications for all Canadians: if every intervenor in every constitutional case were able to claim costs, no one — including rich organizations like the National Citizens' Coalition — could afford to take the chance and launch an action under the Charter of Rights and Freedoms.

Janzen's lawyer applied in 1994 for leave to appeal these rulings before the Supreme Court of Canada. There's a lot at stake. If his leave is rejected, or an appeal is heard but lost, Janzen and the coalition will be forced to drop their case because of the potential cost. If that happens, Janzen will have been denied her right to a trial to determine whether or not her constitutional rights were violated. This will mean unions and provincial labour laws are totally beyond challenge by those they most affect.

While Canada's cash-rich unions can abuse the court system in this way, their biggest pay-off has been support of the New Democrats, and, to a lesser extent, the Parti Québécois. By 1992, union leaders had gained control over three provinces — Ontario, British Columbia, and Saskatchewan — thanks to voter disgust at the Liberals and Tories. From the day these regimes took power, they busied themselves imposing the union agenda onto their electorate. New laws were passed which banned replacement workers, further impeded union decertification, punished managements, forced governments to procure services only from union workers, forced unionization on thousands of civil servants and other workers, and removed restrictions on unionization of certain types of workers such as security guards, among others.

Socialist provincial governments have also passed ridiculous regulations for their union backers. For instance, I bought a 60-watt lamp in 1992 from Canadian Tire and on the instruction sheet it said: "In Quebec, this product must be installed by a qualified electrician." This is a good illustration as to how unions render the country uncompetitive. By the time I hired an electrician costing $30 an hour to "hook up" my $6 lamp, I would have quintupled its costs.

TAKING ON QUEBEC'S CONSTRUCTION UNIONS

Union strategy in Canada has been to bankroll and dominate the policies of socialist parties like the New Democrats. But another socialist party is the Parti Québécois in Quebec, where the NDP is virtually non-existent. Quebec-based unions have forged a close alliance with the Parti and helped further along its separatist as well as socialist agenda. Quebec's unions and separatists have conspired for twenty years to lessen competition from non-union as well as non-Quebec competitors in the lucrative and large construction sector. This has served both union as well as "nationalist" purposes.

There have been recent signs that union power is being eroded somewhat as Canadians across the country stand up for their democratic and economic rights. But a story which gave me huge satisfaction began with a column I wrote in 1992, quoting a letter from an Ottawa reader who was bemoaning the fact that, as a construction worker, he was forced to seek work in Southern Ontario because non-unionized Quebec construction workers, who were not licensed to work at all in their home province, were dominating most of the contracts and subcontracts in Ottawa. He said it was unfair that they could work in Ottawa or elsewhere in Ontario, while he could not go over to Hull or the rest of Quebec and tender for work. I agreed and wrote about it.

A week later, I got a call from a Gatineau, Quebec, entrepreneur named Jocelyn Dumais, who asked to meet with me. He traipsed into the lobby of the posh Château Laurier covered in cement dust and wearing jeans and steel-toed boots. He was charming and funny, and we hit it off immediately. I decided to help and, between us, we certainly changed things.

Through the unflagging efforts of this middle-class business-man from Gatineau, Quebec's Liberals months later did the unthinkable. For the first time in twenty years the government partially deregulated the construction labour market by allowing non-union labour to work without obtaining non-union permits on residential projects.

I cast around for a good angle and exploited the predicament of well-known Quebec boxer Gaeton Hart, winner of three Canadian lightweight championships. After struggling to make a living outside the ring, I wrote, he faced a knock-out punch and jail sentence in Quebec for the crime of working. "Gaeton was the victim — along with thousands of other Quebec workers — of an unholy deal struck nearly 20 years ago between union boss Louis Laberge and then-neophyte politician Robert Bourassa. That deal led to laws which unfairly restrict all construction jobs in Quebec to workers in recognized unions or to those who have obtained permits from the QCC, or Quebec Construction Commission," I wrote in *The Financial Post* and *Ottawa Sun*.

Here was another rub: these laws also prevented other Canadian workers from working in Quebec, even though Quebeckers were free to work anywhere in Canada. In fact, the restrictive union rules and permit system forced many Quebeckers to seek work elsewhere.

Gaeton was a sympathetic case. His carpentry permit lapsed in 1984, and he hadn't been able to get one since. Between boxing bouts, he was caught working without a permit earlier in 1993 by one of the inspectors from Quebec's Construction Commission who prowl the roads looking for people working illegally. Teams of inspectors routinely went on to sites to check for permits or cards. Hart was charged, pleaded not guilty, and was to be tried on February 3. He faced a $300 fine or a jail sentence. He and Jocelyn decided that, to bring publicity to bear on the issue, Gaeton would not pay the fine, but would go to jail.

"I'm going to jail. I'm not paying the fine," Hart told me in an interview from Jocelyn's house. "I had to go on welfare this year while training for my last fight because I wasn't allowed to work. That's not right. I'm not paying a fine just because I want to work."

I found out Gaeton was far from alone. While in Ottawa, I went to Hull's provincial court. The clerks told me that dozens of Quebec workers appeared there every week facing fines or jail sentences for working. They were fined $150 per incident, and their employers $2,600. Figures in 1991 were 25,500 fines levied in Quebec. Fines were so commonplace that one clerk told me the court dealt with them in batches. "Offenders" were regularly scheduled for their first appearances or pleas on Tuesdays, and trials for those pleading not guilty on Wednesdays. Court officials said the workers were ushered in and out by the dozens, like in a routine traffic court. Most firms regarded paying these fines simply as part of the normal cost of doing business.

"Many workers who cannot pay the fine have gone to jail, but most workers pay even though this is totally unfair," said Jocelyn Dumais. He became involved in the issue after returning to his home province after spending eleven years in Windsor, Ontario, as a cement contractor. Looking forward to working in Quebec, he found himself up against the restrictive and unfair system. His company, Linden Footings Limited, had been hit with fines in 1991 of $35,985.58 for employing so-called illegals. He said the system had to change because transgressions of these unjust laws were widespread.

"If you had 150 workers on any construction site in Quebec, I'd guess that half of them would be 'illegals' or working without the permit," he said. "We call inspectors 'boubou macout,' and run like crazy when they arrive. I have hidden in a dumpster for two hours to avoid being caught once. Imagine having to do that just so I can work?"

Jocelyn tried for months to interest the Quebec press and politicians, to no avail. But he kept chipping away, enlisting the help of friends and handing out a business card that read "Travailleurs illegaux Québécois Construction" (or illegal construction workers' association). He also placed ads in Quebec newspapers at his own expense to try to garner support. But politicians — frightened of union goons — wouldn't touch the issue with a barge pole. "We need your help to change things," he said. "The press and politicians in Quebec are too scared to touch this one. *Le Droit* refused an advertisement I wanted in the paper which said: 'Buy from Ontario — support Quebec construction workers.' What do you think of that, as far as freedom of the press?"

Jocelyn said when he came back to Quebec he was denied a permit or worker's card. Then they insulted him. "They sent me an apprentice first-year card and I told them to get lost," he said. "I have seventeen years' experience, and who do they think they are? This system is against the Charter of Rights."

The way Quebec's system worked was that the category mentioned on the permit was important because that dictated the rate of pay and benefits employers had to fork over. "If you pay somebody $22 an hour, and they should be paid $23 an hour, they will give you a big fine," said Jocelyn. "The choice for most workers is to hide to work or go on welfare. What's worst of all is that young people cannot get cards, even after going to college to learn a trade. It's not right, because all the high school drop-outs don't have the chance to do construction work legally."

The Quebec commission still exercises sweeping powers, he said. At a time when he owed $312.37 in unpaid fines, a government official came to Jocelyn's home, inspected his possessions, and a week later sent a notice indicating that if the fines weren't paid Dumais's twenty-eight-inch television and microwave oven would be seized. He paid.

My sympathetic article about Gaeton Hart and Jocelyn's cause netted publicity in Ottawa and Hull newspapers, and appearances on open-line radio shows. Jocelyn also acquired more supporters, and several of them crashed union meetings and political gatherings and held press conferences to make their point. It was fortunate for Quebec construction workers, as well as for Quebec consumers, that Jocelyn got mad enough to challenge Quebec's laws.

I told him we could make the biggest splash when Gaeton or someone else was carted off to jail for working in front of television and newspaper cameras. Our chance came on January 15, 1993, when one of his friends, David Giroux, refused to pay $1,800 in fines and decided to go to jail. I got on the phone immediately, calling the *Ottawa Sun*, CTV, CBC, and two radio stations in Ottawa. I sold them on the story. They arrived. But somebody mysteriously paid Giroux's $1,800 fine, so he didn't have to go to jail in front of the cameras. "We don't know if it was a Quebec union or the government who didn't want him to go to jail because of how it would look," explained Jocelyn.

Jocelyn's agitation was critical to the success of his crusade, but the biggest breakthrough came when an important *Post* reader — New Brunswick premier Frank McKenna — read my article about Gaeton and then took up the cause. My article also mentioned another case involving New Brunswick entrepreneur Randy Brown, who, like Jocelyn, had been unfairly discriminated against and financially damaged as a result of Quebec's labour restrictions. Brown, owner of a kitchen supply company in Saint John, New Brunswick, launched a legal challenge under the Charter of Rights and Freedoms, suing after his workers were forced off a construction site in Montreal in 1991. His firm was run out of town, even though it had won the contract to install new countertops it had manufactured for a large Montreal Holiday Inn.

"We're unionized and were given the go-ahead, but after one week on the job we were told 'foreigners' couldn't work in the province," said Brown in a telephone interview. "My workers were verbally harassed, tools and machines were kicked, and we were physically threatened by union workers. At the same time the construction commission inspectors forced us to hire four Quebec workers and hit us with fines."

Brown's lawsuit alleged the delays cost his firm $38,000, and fines were another $19,900. That plus other damages and costs add up to $91,000. The suit maintains that the laws were illegal because the charter guarantees "livelihood mobility."

Premier McKenna announced that his government would examine the Brown case and others closely. It did, and New Brunswick passed in its legislature exactly the same restrictions Quebec had erected against its neighbours: bans against work or tendering by outsiders. The City of Ottawa followed suit, and so did Ontario Premier Bob Rae months later. Under extreme pressure outside and inside the province, Quebec's Liberals partially deregulated the construction labour market in 1993 and in 1994 signed reciprocal, open-market trade and labour agreements with neighbouring provinces.

The extraordinary power of the unions in Quebec had brought about an unjust situation, which a feisty French Canadian turned around by pure grit and determination. But, for years, these practices have cost Quebec consumers huge amounts of money and forced ordinary workers without union cards to go without work, or to work on the sly, as though they were criminals. While it appears to have been sorted out, the facts are that union power still remains a problem in Quebec, and its deregulation was only partial. Besides, any new government can revert to the bad old ways of the past in a flash.

THE BATTLE JOINED IN ENGLISH CANADA

Doug Gammie of Oshawa, Ontario, took on Goliath. Through his efforts, and those of other autoworkers, he was able to sever the financial ties between his local — the Canadian Auto Workers' largest affiliated branch — and the New Democratic Party. The eventual triumph at this local and a handful of others in Ontario would be a harbinger for the humiliating defeat suffered by the New Democrats in the 1993 federal election. Reduced to just nine seats, it became obvious that the party could no longer reconcile the various fringe interests it had stitched together into a party. Unionized miners and foresters were upset at its tough environmental stances. Autoworkers like Gammie were upset with the New Democrat's deficits, tax gouges, and anti–free trade stance when they knew their well-paid jobs depended upon business with the United States. Others disliked its support for abortion; employment equity, which discriminates against white males; gay rights; day-care support; and other measures.

"I've never been an NDP supporter, and most of the people in the plant aren't either," said Gammie in an interview in March 1993. He and others formed a committee that collected 8,000 signatures on a petition calling for an end to any links with the NDP. "My pet issue has always been that CAW power is being used to pursue agendas often the same as the NDP's. This CAW power is not coming from the membership, even though the membership is being used to back it up."

Naturally, CAW national president Buzz Hargrove and other union leaders were furious, and dubbed Gammie's action as a case of "being outflanked by right-wing bastards."

But Gammie, an articulate and thoughtful university graduate and GM millwright, puts the lie to that. This is about democracy, he said. "People see through that [view]. The union here tried desperately to say: 'NDP contributions were only a couple of dollars every year, so what's the big deal?' We said: 'No CAW power should be used in a way we the members don't want it used.' The workers understand that. It's our money, and we don't know how much is involved because much is kept very secret. It's our power that's being used to further an agenda."

I interviewed another petitioner — Sam Zahara in Windsor, Ontario — who agreed that workers had been kept in the dark for too long by their union leaders. He said many of his workers were upset they were helping the NDP. He collected 1,000 signatures from workers at his GM transmission plant in just three days. They also demanded a referendum on support of the NDP. "We want the right to an in-plant vote when it comes to supporting political parties. We do not want a handful of people at a Sunday general membership meeting to make our decisions for us.

"Our last increase in union dues went for NDP campaigning

129

in Nova Scotia. We didn't know that. So many people in our plant, when they heard their dues were going to the NDP, were really upset. I don't even know how much of my dues goes every month. It's tons of money," he said.

Harold Reid, a retired CAW worker in Oshawa, told me that millions were siphoned indirectly to the NDP through unions' contributions to organizations like the Ontario Federation of Labour and the Canadian Labour Congress. "If the rank and file only knew the half of it, they'd get quite a shock. We have this political action committee, and the union paid three guys their lost wages for six weeks to go door-to-door handing out pamphlets for the mayor of Whitby, Ontario, an NDPer."

GM has to let people off work "for union business," he explained. "The company has no choice, and we pay their lost wages. But handing out pamphlets [and] running around the streets of Whitby to get some socialist elected is not union business. This is something the membership doesn't know. I can't think of one single job any of this has created. I can say how many jobs this has lost. But our unions are run by individuals who want to further their own political careers. They are not serving the rank and file."

Besides contributing manpower, the union gives NDP candidates the use of union vehicles, printed materials, advertising, and facilities for rallies. "I had to pay $400 to rent the union hall for my kids' weddings, but NDP candidates get it for nothing," Reid said.

In May 1993, Gammie's efforts bore fruit, and the referendum vote supported the severing of all ties with the NDP. Another plant, outside London, Ontario, also voted to boot out party contributions. Workers there were upset that NDP leader Audrey McLaughlin had opposed Canada's participation in the Gulf War. The plant made vehicle parts for the

Canadian armed forces. But Sam Zahara was stymied in his efforts. An unidentified "company official" ordered him to stop circulating his petition and, lacking enough names, he was denied the chance to put a referendum to the vote at an executive meeting.

But the biggest victory against union oppression was won in Alberta. The deregulation of labour markets in Alberta was part of a massive and painful correction that the province underwent after the triple whammy in the 1980s. In rapid succession, the province was hit by a recession, the confiscatory National Energy Program with its new taxes on oil and natural-gas production, and the collapse of oil prices in 1986 to as little as US$14 a barrel from US$36 a barrel, and gas prices along with it. Calgary, the oil capital of Canada, went from being a city bursting with development to one where bankruptcies, project stoppages, and serious unemployment were the order of the day. Many of the easterners who had migrated to Alberta to benefit as unskilled labourers during the oil boom returned home to joblessness in Newfoundland or Ontario.

Because of twelvefold price hikes by the oil cartel, Alberta's oil industry and the industries and businesses it supported were living in a fool's paradise. Wages, prices, house and land values went through the roof because of a generalized, but misguided belief that the boom would never end. When it did end, some 80 per cent of the province's construction industry was unionized and saddled with excessively high labour costs.

Non-union shops stole what little business was left. The unionized shops, which had dominated the industry, lobbied the legislature for changes to laws and got them. Reforms included the right to set up or buy a parallel, non-union shop which undermined the unionized labour pool. Then, in 1988, the province passed "secret ballot" legislation which created a two-step process for certification. If a union obtained 40 per cent support among workers, workers were entitled to a secret ballot vote by all members. A majority was needed to certify. Similarly, it became easier to decertify a union. The result is that employers and workers alike have the freedom to choose. Contractors can own both union and non-union outfits. Workers can belong to unions, pay dues, and work for non-union outfits.

"The Alberta Labour Relations Board has said as long as the union can't offer him another job they cannot fine the member for working for a non-union shop," explained Steve Kushner, executive director of Merit Contractors' Association Inc., an employer group which sprung up in Alberta and else-where following reforms. When asked whether it was possible to set up workers by luring them with union jobs away from non-union ones, then firing them, he said: "Politically that's difficult because unions can't let one individual jump the hiring call list."

The result is that Alberta has become Canada's first right-to-work province. Not surprisingly, its labour rates and costs are among the country's lowest, and a change was needed to help cushion the blows sustained by Albertans during the difficult 1980s. It remains an incredible success story that through technological innovations in the oil industry and a massive labour-market correction in the province, Alberta was able to prosper on prices that were less than half what they had been just a decade earlier.

Kushner pointed out that union leaders are not necessarily even devoted to the principle of unionism. In construction, for example, they are often power-hungry monopolists serving

American interests. "All of Canada's construction trade unions are headquartered in Washington, D.C. They are American unions, not Canadian ones. And they hate the alternative unions, like the Christian Labor Association, Canadian Iron Industry Union, or General Workers Union. These organizations are sometimes spread across sectors or trades, or sometimes just include all the workers in a specific company," he said.

Unions are also ruthless when challenged, employing the type of goon and gangster tactics that their American gangster founders were famous for during the 1930s and 1940s south of the border. The most tragic recent incident involved several union members charged with murder in Yellowknife for allegedly planting a bomb that killed eight "scab" or replacement workers underground during a lengthy strike. Violent incidents are not unusual in Canada by unionists.

For instance, in 1994 a woman contractor in Nova Scotia decided to organize a lobby group to fight for legislation following an unjustifiable court decision which ruled that only unionized labour could ever be used in the province for government work. Their lobbying effort was successful. The Liberal government there agreed to pass legislation overturning the decision. Inspired by their success the group decided to push for more labour law reforms to open up the province.

"They called themselves the Right to Work Association in Nova Scotia, and they asked us to participate in a seminar," said Kushner. "They had a room ready in a downtown hotel to accommodate 120 people, and at 8:00 a.m., as we were gathering to go inside, about 100 union guys arrived all liquored-up to disrupt proceedings. A few shouted as they entered the room, '$100 to the guy who gives the first punch.' The RCMP were there and did nothing, and we couldn't get into that room to start our seminar after the shoving and excitement until 2:00 p.m. that afternoon."

Unions have been known to abuse their pension funds to shore up their situation. Some unions have attempted to levy an hourly fee from their members to subsidize union jobs. Both practices are unethical, if not illegal. Workers could challenge trustees of any pension fund which subsidized union bids on the basis that trustees were not fulfilling their only fiduciary obligation, which is to maximize the value of the pension savings to ensure future benefits for contributors. The other issue raised is one involving favouritism: which union jobs would unions with pension or worker funds subsidize and why?

Canada needs laws to uphold the principle of voluntary unionism. People should have a right to organize without interference. Right-to-work legislation in the United States has its problems too. But the goal should be voluntary unionization: workers should always have a choice as to which union they may want to join, if any. As things stand, they are sometimes forced to join unions who take their money and squander it on unpopular or unknown secret agendas or dirty tricks.

VINCE'S TALE

Vince Cutruzzola, a smallish electrician with a high school education, came to see me in 1993. He originally didn't want his real name used because he was afraid of harassment from the electrical workers' union. His story is not unique: there are thousands of tradesmen in Ontario, British Columbia, and elsewhere whose right to earn a living has been unjustly curbed by union-inspired labour laws.

Vince is a small-time operator. A good electrician, he employs others from time to time, depending upon the size of the job he is working on. Most of the time, he's a sole practitioner, estimating, organizing, and doing the work. In 1990, he got a lead on some work involving construction of a shopping mall. It was a unionized job, meaning that only union shops could bid. Vince joined the union so that he could bid for the work. He told me he was assured by the union that he could opt out of membership later if he decided to. He won the contract, hired three unionized electricians, and finished the job. Then he wrote a letter to the union, calling it quits, and thought that was that.

It wasn't. For three years he worked around the province as a non-union outfit, but the union finally caught up with him. They took him to the Ontario Labour Relations Board, saying that he was operating "illegally," circumventing laws that required him to hire only union labour. His lawyer told him that he either had been misled or had misunderstood, and that he could not opt out of the union merely by writing a letter. His union employees had to vote in favour of decertification. "But I told him I didn't have any employees any more, and I didn't have those employees any more, so how could I hold a vote?" he said.

Because there were, in fact, no employees, the lawyer told him he had a 50–50 chance of winning his case. If he lost the case, he stood to lose $200,000 in fines, plus legal fees. Facing financial ruin, he capitulated, and signed on as a union shop a second time. He should not have done this, but he should also not have been forced into the position where his only choices were catastrophic.

In essence, Vince must run a union shop forever, even though union wages, by 1994, were double what the market would pay. He said this was unfair. In essence, he has been condemned to perpetual unemployment because union wage rates are uncompetitive and most jobs must be tendered based on non-union rates. He was also told by his lawyer that he could not change the name of his company or work as an "employee" of a shell company owned by a friend or relative; if he did so, unions would dog him and take him to the labour board under the "key man" provisions of the Labour Act. "Key man" provisions stipulate that, if someone is essentially running the show, he or she cannot hide behind the ownership of someone else and pretend to be an employee.

His only options are to work underground, to work as an employee in a non-union shop, to leave the province, or to abandon his trade. In essence, labour laws have deprived Vince of the ability to support himself. An unsympathetic labour lawyer said of his case: "He can go to another province and start a non-union firm. He can become another tradesman non-union. But he gave up his right to operate a non-union business as an electrical contractor in the province."

Vince responded: "I don't want to move. I don't want to do anything else. I don't have the financial backing to be a union shop. They only get the large jobs. All my options are illegal. If I change my name, the whole thing starts over again. And I'm told if I'm caught the fines are $50 an hour for every non-union hour me and my guys work. That would ruin me. I have to work and I'll have to do it by hiding. I don't believe this is happening to me in Canada."

Just months after meeting with Vince and trying to help him, I got a call from Toronto lawyer Ron Himelfarb, who had another tragic story involving the electricians' union. His uncle, Eli Himelfarb, was facing financial ruin as a result of Ontario labour laws. Between 1972 and 1975, Eli Himelfarb was a minor partner in a contracting business that hired union men. The company, which eventually went out of business, had never formally signed a collective agreement with a union. Himelfarb worked from 1975 to 1982 as a union electrician doing odd jobs, mostly outside his province.

Then, in 1982, he was laid off and decided to start his own electrical service business. He gradually built up his contacts, and by 1984 was incorporated and employing three or four electricians at a time. But, in December 1993, a complaint was made by the International Brotherhood of Electrical Workers to the Ontario Labour Relations Board, which led to a four-day hearing in February 1994. The union wanted dues on all wages Himelfarb's company had paid from 1984 to 1992.

"We are in dire straits," said his wife, Mary Ellen Himelfarb. "It has cost us $15,000 in legal fees, and it will destroy us. It is destroying us. We feel it was unjust because there was a great deal of time between when he was hiring union guys and now. Before the hearing, we wanted to settle with the union, but they wanted us to hire union men for a job we were doing which we had bid at non-union wages. Union wages are 250 per cent higher. Helpers wanted $23 an hour to make coffee. They didn't accept our counteroffer. They just would not let us off the hook and they said there is no figure we could pay them to make up for all the years we didn't pay.

"The union is arguing that there was 'succession,' that his new business was really the old business, or that he merely continued the business from 1975 to 1982 and therefore was just trying to get around the laws," she added. "But that's crazy. My husband is fifty-six and I'm fifty-four and they've just taken away our life. We're both suffering from depression. The union thing hangs over our heads like a guillotine. He spends his days moping and drinking. Is this Russia? It's horrendous taking away a man's opportunities. Let the man work. Let him try to make a living. This is just hell."

The Himelfarbs faced personal bankruptcy if the board ruled in the union's favour, and there is absolutely no appeal from the decision. There is also no constitutional protection because provincial labour laws are exempt from constitutional provisions. And there is no legislative jurisdiction such as the Competitions Act because union monopolies and anti-competitive activities are exempt from the act. They lost their case in spring 1994.

MORE PRIVATE-SECTOR OPPRESSION

One upsetting story I wrote about in May 1994 involved Toromont Industries Ltd., a company listed on the Toronto Stock Exchange, whose shareholders were, in my opinion, victims of Bob Rae's pro-union government. Toromont has the sales and service franchise for Caterpillar Corporation. I suggested shareholders should sue for damages, and police should be involved.

Toromont had $180 million in sales and 575 employees working in sales, service, and maintenance. Of this total, there were 152 unionized mechanics and warehouse staffers who are members of the Canadian Auto Workers (CAW) union. On March 7, 1994, the CAW struck against the company over so-called contract language issues, said Toromont spokesman Al Schoening.

Once a strike starts, Ontario's Bill 40 kicks in, as would similar laws in B.C., Saskatchewan, and Quebec. Under this legislation, companies are forbidden to hire replacements during strikes. Their managers or supervisors perform their functions during the strike, which is what Toromont has been doing since the strike began.

One of Toromont's customers sent me a fax about what the CAW was up to during its strike against Toromont. He was appalled, and so was I. The union had been approaching Toromont's customers and offering to send out striking workers to do maintenance at cut rates during the strike.

"Dear valued customer," began the union fax. "Our team of highly skilled and trained members are prepared to offer you their services during this dispute at very reasonable rates. These are the same people you have trusted and dealt with over the past years to repair your equipment. We thank you for your patience. Signed the BARGAINING committee."

So what we had here was a workforce that was purposely undercutting, and therefore undermining, its employer.

I called the CAW and got Fizul Kerim, plant chair for the union. He did not see the injustice. "If the employer were to replace our work while we're on strike, he'd be breaking the law, but we're replacing own own work," he said. "And we're offering more reasonable rates compared to the company."

So how much of a bargain are you offering your workers' employer's customers? I asked. "Toromont charges time out at around $79 an hour. Our mechanics will be prepared to charge the customer a negotiated rate of $50 an hour, or else a flat fee. They know how many hours these jobs take, so they can quote a flat-fee figure," said Kerim.

Don't they understand, I wrote, that if Toromont charged only $50 an hour instead of $79 an hour, they could not possibly earn the $29-worth of fancy benefits that they currently pulled in? Didn't they understand that they were proving that they were overpaid and ran the risk of convincing Toromont's customers to permanently use non-unionized mechanics who charged $50 an hour instead of Toromont's $79 an hour?

I told Ontario's Labour minister about this situation, and his spokesman would not comment, except to say: "There are rules about subcontracting, but we're not in a position to say whether what's going on is, or isn't, in compliance because it is conceivable this could come before the Labour Relations Board."

Fat chance of that. The company was concentrating on settling the labour dispute and didn't want to take on the union goons and their high-priced legal help. Besides, businesses know these labour boards are biased. The fact that Ontario's Labour ministry was copping out was hardly surprising, considering that the minister, Bob MacKenzie, is a former union organizer and shamelessly pro-union. It was obvious that the CAW was circumventing the law by providing "replacement workers."

I also brought the matter to the attention of the Ontario attorney general because customer lists are the property of their owners and therefore confidential. I suggested that the union leaders may be in unlawful possession of Toromont's customer list — guilty of theft. I argued that police should be involved in the case.

Finally I said Toromont's shareholders should sue the union for damages, and their board of directors should consider serving its Ontario customers from New York or Ohio until Ontario elected a government that believed in free enterprise. The strike would be settled, but the province would never lift a finger to help Toromont.

PUBLIC-SECTOR BATTLES

While private-sector unionism wanes and faces challengers, Canada's powerful public-sector unions remain an enormous impediment to the country's economic efficiency. Some civil servants are trying to change things from the inside, trying to make their unions more democratic. Their stories illustrate the problems they face.

Paul Vidlak worked during the federal civil service strike in 1991 and was "suspended" from membership in the Public Service Alliance of Canada (PSAC) for five years for being a "scab." He does not feel it is right that he should be punished by a union he never wanted to join in the first place over his failure to support a strike he disagreed with. "I was suspended from membership, even though I never signed a union card," he said. "But I still have to pay dues."

If Vidlak revealed a bias against labour by crossing a picket line, surely those who manned the line revealed a bias against management? But no letters criticizing the strikers were sent by union officials. Besides the faulty logic, imagine a union collecting dues from an individual, and then purposely, and out of pique, trying to sabotage the man's career by calling him "biased."

It's also outrageous that Vidlak — because of the Rand Formula — was forced to pay dues to a union which was out to get him. Why, in light of the fact that he had been kicked out of a union, did he have to pay dues? Why did he have to contribute to a union which had cut him off from certain benefits, such as going to bat for him in grievances? It was unfair, but Canada's unjust Rand Formula dictates that workers must pay dues, even if they are not union members.

Vidlak wrote to his "employer" — the federal government

— requesting the freedom to opt out of paying dues. "The Rand Formula is a 1946 antiquated piece of legislation. The rationale after the Second World War was that unions needed legislative protection. I questioned that thinking then and now much more so," he wrote. "Canada is a signator to the International Labor Organization Convention 87 which guarantees employees the right to establish and join organizations of their own choosing. I submit to you, sir, that implicit in this right to join is also the right not to join any organization. I did not freely choose to join and pay dues to the PSAC. The provision in our current collective agreement for automatic union membership and dues deduction would appear to be in violation of Canada's signature on the U.N. document and a violation of international law."

The reply by then Treasury Board head Gilles Loiselle was interesting, if questionable. "Though I recognize that the current regime is not without problems, I nevertheless view our system as a delicate balance between the rights of individuals and those of the collectivity. The Freedom of Association Committee of the International Labor Organization agrees that union security clauses freely negotiated between employers and unions breach neither ILO conventions which deal with employees' rights to join unions and the payment of dues."

Another civil servant who crossed the line, Joseph Degrandmont, took another route in protesting union power. He formed with others the Humanistic League, devoted to issues of ethics, morality, and free will. Their strategy was based on a precedent set in 1993 involving a Parks Canada employee who was allowed to divert his dues to a charity for reasons of conscience. Degrandmont wants to give his dues to the United Way.

"A few dozen of us want to divert our dues to charities too.

We do not want to pay dues at all to that union because we have no choice and our organization believes in free will," he said. "The union leadership is entirely dictatorial, membership has no voice, union leaders can declare million-dollar campaigns against the Progressive Conservative party. Not that we're Conservatives, but we are tired of our money being used without our permission as to its use."

Bringing about democratic reforms or responsiveness is difficult because of the way the union is structured, he said. "The union is structured on the basis of the Communist Party system. People elect members of one cell, but cell members elect members to the next cell level, and so on to the top. So the guy at the bottom has no say at all in terms of what the guy at the top is doing. In effect, unions are dictatorships and hard to move. You can join it and run for office, but one individual cannot move it from the inside.

"Since Rand came down with his ruling, the union has grown and become unresponsive to the needs or wishes of members. Yet we are unfairly obligated to financially support this dictatorship group that does not ask us how they may use our funds, whether they can raise fees, whether they can get into debt, or whether we should even go on strike. They tell us nothing, and no one knows how many civil servants went on strike and how many actually refused to strike. [PSAC president Daryl] Bean threatened to publish the scabs' names, and I submit that would constitute the first referendum against his union."

Degrandmont said he expected to be punished in some way by the union's radicals because he went public with his interview in *The Financial Post*. "But this union represents such a grave social injustice that I'm willing to put up with the intimidation. I chose not to respect the strike because my opinion was not even requested. It was all a Daryl Bean ego trip. And even though I'm working in a different building, some people still give me dirty looks."

Another victim of union harassment was federal civil servant Ernie Forsen, vice-president of his union local, who crossed the picket line during the strike. He took PSAC to small-claims court to try and get his dues back. The court dismissed his petition for jurisdictional reasons. As usual, it was a David-and-Goliath situation. Forsen had to represent himself in court. The union hired an expensive lawyer, paid for, in part, by Forsen's dues.

Forsen did not strike because there was no reason to. "Making children work in mines is something to strike for, but you don't go on strike if you are decently paid, have four weeks' holiday, fringe benefits, good pension plans," he said. "You go on strike if it's a question of survival, or if you have the backing of the vast majority of membership."

Forsen had been a vice-president of the union in the past and had some insight about how things work from the inside. "I was suspended simply because I went to work. They didn't like that. I was a vice-president of the local, and they made sure they got me. I did not strike because it was the only way to get some attention to change union leadership. Daryl Bean is living twenty-five years in the past, when you had to go on strike. The average worker cannot question the big boys. It's an undemocratic type of organization, and the leaders are fat cats with big salaries and perks."

Forsen said union delegates at a convention decided to go the strike route without consulting members at large. A union spokesman said that was true, but added that any bargaining unit within the union could have forced a vote with the support of a majority of members. No unit did. Forsen admitted there is apathy as well as fear.

"Many people I work with just stayed home. They didn't work because they are afraid of the union, and they didn't picket either. For me it's a question of whether you're going to let bully boys mistreat you, and what kind of a society we live in. People yelled at me going through the picket line. That's the sort of thing kids do," he said.

Union power plays still continue, particularly with NDP regimes in three provinces. Bob Rae's government handed over 13,000 management-level civil servants on a platter to one of his party's biggest contributors, the Ontario Public Service Employees Union (OPSEU). They were worth about $800 each per year in union dues. Rae indirectly abused his public trust by giving $10 million a year in dues to a supporter. The civil servants were never even given the choice of voting for a union or choosing what union to vote for. Rae's excuse was simply that the percentage of unionized workers in the province was below the national average.

The decision paid off for Rae in spring 1994 when a grateful OPSEU agreed to let Rae skim several hundred millions of dollars out of their employee pension funds to reduce that year's provincial deficit. Other unions, notably the one representing the provincial police, balked because the pension funds were not in a surplus situation. In fact, said a police spokesman, the government had passed legislation two years earlier to top up the funds because of massive unfunded liabilities over the years. This manoeuvre with union help was another example of how the New Democrats in power simply work to broaden and enhance the privileges of unions over workers.

THE ECONOMIC COSTS

Unionization has been very damaging to Canada's economy, with respect to both private and public sectors. James Bursey, an Ontario-based entrepreneur and consultant specializing in "metal bashing" industries, says he has moved as many as 8,000 jobs to the United States since 1986. He works on companies that are in trouble and need turning around. He and his partners also own three Ontario manufacturing companies, which had $14.5 million in sales in 1992 with 165 workers in the auto, moulding, and machining fields. He says unions and taxes are causing the deindustrialization of the country.

"In Windsor, in 1991, the mould-making industry alone lost nine shops, all due to union problems. A total of twenty closed, nine due to union trouble, and the other eleven left for financial reasons or to go to the U.S," he said. "New labour laws make survival more difficult for small and medium-sized manufacturers. So do government deficits. Small businesses are fighting to borrow money from banks in competition with their own governments. Big companies can borrow offshore at lower rates of interest, but not the smaller ones." One of the worst culprits, he said, is the Canadian Auto Workers. "They are unrealistic and have a political, not an economic agenda, for their members. I have not found them willing to listen to reason, with a few exceptions. At the national level, they are ideologues not businessmen."

By contrast, he said, the U.S. counterpart, the United Auto Workers, is business-like. "The UAW realizes it is selling units of labour and makes sure purchasers of units of labour pay the highest prices possible without ruining their businesses. I can deal with the UAW anytime."

Tragically, he said, the workers are caught in the middle,

often losing their jobs when a plant closes due to union intransigence. Worse yet, unionization has essential flaws, and works at odds with free enterprise.

"The biggest problem is defining management prerogatives. What can you ask workers to do? What areas can they work in? Can you move them around at will? In the more entrenched shops, there is no flexibility, no ability to move, so they carry lots of dead wood. With a seniority system, you must use the longest survivors, who are not always the best. That's the inherent flaw in any union shop, and if people don't think that costs money, they should run a unionized shop."

In 1992 he worked on a turn-around of a Peterborough, Ontario, company and said it was a horror story. "This is the great Canadian workforce that Bob Rae talks about. About 18 per cent of them were illiterate. There was 25 per cent absenteeism daily, and during the opening of hunting or fishing season, 76 per cent were absent. We had to shut down. Five hundred jobs gone."

The story is the same in the public sector, as I discovered by comparing a public school board in Peel Region west of Toronto with one in Calgary. Both areas were roughly the same size, and the socio-economic profile of their residents was similar. While such comparisons are never perfect, I believe that this one comes about as close to an apple-to-apple comparison as possible. And what it reveals to taxpayers is that reasonably good education can be delivered in a more efficient and cheaper way. It also puts the lie to union arguments that, by paying teachers higher wages and lowering pupil–teacher ratios, education will be improved. Calgary shows that is not the case at all, and the union arguments are simply designed to increase union dues.

The Calgary Board of Education has about 97,000 students. Peel Region has 93,893. Calgary students score as well in national or other testing as do Peel students, in fact slightly higher in maths and sciences. Students from both regions are accepted as equals in terms of university admissions. Their standards are roughly the same.

But consider the differences to taxpayers. Both teaching workforces are unionized, but Peel's has been more successful at getting funds out of the public. Calgary was spending around $5,528 per student a year on education from kinder-garten to the end of secondary school. Peel spent $6,738 per elementary student and $7,770 per secondary school student. This represented a huge cost difference without any huge differences in terms of the "end product."

The added costs were almost entirely attributable to the fact that Peel's unions obtained more wages for less work than did Calgary's unions. A teacher with twelve years of experience in Peel makes $66,776 a year. That's equivalent, in the private sector, where people work twelve months a year, to an annualized salary of $73,740. If you add to that job security and an excessively generous pension that sometimes kicks in at age fifty-five years or before, Peel's teachers represent an unnecessary overhead.

By contrast, Calgary's twelve-year veterans make $57,645 a year and live in a region with a similar cost of living. They also deliver more for their money, and provide 190 days of instruction per year for students. Peel not only overpays its teachers but gives the kids only 185 days per year of instruction. Conclusion: One-third of Canada's workers are caught in a system without choice. They must contribute to causes they may not believe in but which their union supports. About one-third of them must contribute cash to American unions, which often have not reinvested pension and other proceeds proportionately in Canada. They must submit to the decisions made by unions which are not democratically constituted. Secret ballots for strike mandates, annual membership tests, or referendums on policy and strategic initiatives among members are unheard of.

Even worse is what unions do to the country's work ethic, particularly in the public sector. Unions force employers to pay workers identical rates of pay if they have served the same number of years. Seniority, not merit, is the rule, and this is soul-destroying to those with more initiative or ambition. The result is that excellent teachers and nurses are paid the same wages as mediocre ones. Ambitious employees can get greater rewards only by seeking promotion to managerial positions. Alternatively, they can decide to work less hard, knowing that their pay will remain the same as if they made a greater effort. The result is that the public sector is bloated with managers who have been promoted in order to be better rewarded and is filled with many workers who do as little as possible to enhance their earnings.

Their unions fiercely resist attempts to give good workers merit pay, to exclude managers from paying dues, or to introduce bonus schemes. Instead, the country has a demoralized public-sector workforce who have no incentive to cut costs, save taxpayers money, or work harder. That so many of them do work hard is a testimony to the basic work ethic, and pride, of most Canadians.

Unions act to impede discipline within workforces by providing a "grievance" procedure which is, in my experience, often greatly abused. Workers from minority groups routinely run to their unions, crying about discrimination, when their pay is docked or they are laid off and disciplined. Others use

149

the grievance process to get even with managers they dislike. I have personally known of instances where disgruntled unionized workers filed a grievance against their managers for being asked to work overtime, being asked to take on some of the responsibilities of an absent colleague, being asked to work a different shift, being asked to do things differently, or being asked to work harder.

While most union workers don't indulge in such shenanigans, a great deal of damage is done by union leaders just doing their jobs well. Unions, by definition, must justify their existence — and earn their dues — by holding out for the highest wages they can possibly get, using whatever means are available. Once a well-heeled or weak employer caves in and establishes that upper-end wage scale, the rest of the industry is whipsawed and forced to pay high wages, regardless of market conditions. This guarantees lay-offs and has cost more Canadians more jobs than cheap imports from Asia ever did.

The resistance to lower labour prices by unions flies in the face of marketplace realities: labour rates must fluctuate downward as well as upward along with corporate profits, rents, currencies, and commodity prices. Rigid labour rates force businesses to buy offshore, automate, leave, or shut down. Canada's closed-shop economy has contributed to its deindustrialization. The same thing has occurred in Europe and the United States. The closed shop has also led to a decline in union membership in the private sector in Canada to match American levels.

But Canada's union movement is most powerful in the public sector, and its power will impede the type of government restructuring that is required in order to reduce deficits and to ensure the nation's future viability. There are some positive signs that public-sector union leaders are losing their grip. Faced with massive cuts to balance the budget, Alberta's public-sector unions took to the streets in mass rallies and media campaigns. But, by spring 1994, their leaders were embarrassed because the turnout was tiny in relation to their union membership. Similarly, the Public Service Alliance of Canada strike in 1991 among federal civil servants was undermined by the 5,000 or so civil servants who crossed picket lines. Tens of thousands more were not sympathetic to the strike and simply stayed home.

The signs of rebellion are there, but the arsenal of weapons available to unions, including the New Democrats and Parti Québécois, still remain in the absence of new laws. Alberta, as usual, showed that the way was not that difficult and certainly did not have to involve constitutional revisions — a near-impossibility in Canada.

Alberta is the only province which has replaced forced unionism with "voluntary unionism." This sea-change occurred in 1988 with legislation that allowed unionized employers to operate non-union shops too. The Alberta reforms were the result of a wrenching recession in the early 1980s and the collapse of oil prices in 1986. These massive market "corrections" forced businesses in the province to take Draconian measures in order to survive. Construction came to a standstill, companies laid off thousands of employees, exploratory drilling nearly ended, house prices fell, and wage roll-backs in companies were commonplace. Even so, there were thousands of personal and corporate bankruptcies, and the province's heavily unionized construction sector was very badly hurt.

Contractors began to plead to the province for relief. Calgary, for instance, had fifty office-tower cranes dominating its skyline as a result of twelve-fold increases in oil prices throughout the 1970s. Oil companies spent massive amounts of money in the belief that prices would continue to skyrocket. In an atmosphere in which money was no object, unionized contractors flourished.

By the time the bottom fell out, some 80 per cent of construction workers were in unions, and their wage rates rendered them unemployable. Construction slowed to a trickle, and the government was forced to either change the labour laws or push most of its contractors out of business. So, in 1988, it allowed non-union shops and undertook other measures designed to restore flexibility in labour rates according to market conditions.

The policies worked. And now Alberta workers can belong to a union or not. They can also remain union members while working for a non-union shop. Even more important, the Alberta government is the only government in Canada which protects such workers from union harassment, fines, or other forms of punishment.

The proper role of government is to protect individuals from oppression by wealthy and powerful lobbies or organizations such as unions. Voluntary unionism is a goal to which every enlightened country should aspire. It protects equally those who want to organize and those who don't. But, as things stand in Canada, unions have been conceded special privileges, including the ability to transgress individual freedoms. This is not only unjust in a democracy, but is hobbling our economy and reducing our competitiveness as a nation.

CANADA'S POLITE OPPRESSION

MERICANS DROVE THE LATE RICHARD NIXON OUT OF the U.S. presidency, the world's most powerful office. British parliamentarians have been known to resign over revelations about the tiniest peccadillo. But, in Canada, in 1994 constituents in Scarborough, Ontario, could not remove as their member of Parliament Jag Bhaduria, even though he had misled the public about his credentials in campaign literature and threatened to harm physically a former employer.

Bhaduria's only "punishment" was the pressure which led to his resignation from the Liberal caucus. There was no move made by the ruling Liberals to have him impeached or removed from Parliament. There was no mechanism which would allow his constituents to force a by-election. And no amount of picketing, petitioning, or dreadful publicity could budge him. In Canada, a man like Bhaduria, totally unfit for public office, can hang tough and collect his $64,400 a year salary, $21,300 tax-free expense allowance, and perquisites such as dozens of free flights per year, privileged access to medical care, and a fat pension equivalent to 30 per cent of his average salary. Even though he ran under the Liberal banner, the party washed its hands of him and left constituents stuck with a totally unacceptable representative. They claimed nothing further could be done. That isn't true. They have the power to legislate.

Such arrogance infuriates taxpayers, but they are as powerless to bring in reforms as they are to get governments to reduce their spending. Millions of taxpayers are also frustrated and enraged by government mismanagement of the public sector, its increasing encroachment on individual freedoms, and its incessant constitutional navel-gazing. Despite all the energy that has been expended on the constitution and charter, Canadians are left without protection for their rights. This is ironic, considering that Canada has signed U.N. and other international protocols which guarantee property rights, linguistic rights, and the right of workers to associate freely — or not. These documents were signed to protect Canadian nationals in other, less-enlightened countries, and yet our own governments have failed to protect us from property, linguistic, and union abuses.

The result has been damage to our economy, tax evasion, and a resoundingly negative electorate. It has been said that elections are not won, but lost. This has never been more pertinent than in Canada in the 1990s. In 1992 and 1993, the public rose up and twice rejected the country's mainstream political élite. The first blow was struck when 53 per cent of Canadians voted "no" to the Charlottetown Accord. The second was when two new, alternative parties — Reform and the Bloc Québécois — won 106 seats in the federal election. Reform came in second in another forty or so ridings in Ontario alone, despite its shoestring campaign budget of $1.5 million. By contrast, the Tories spent $10 million and were virtually obliterated. Same with the New Democrats, and their labour agenda. In fact, the Liberals were able to form a majority government only because so many disgruntled Tories voted for Reform in Ontario, which had the effect of splitting the vote.

Canada has been mismanaged so badly by its politicians and bureaucrats that it is burdened by a monstrous, and potentially nation-threatening, debt. Even so, public demands to attack the problem continued to be ignored. In February 1994, the Liberal government handed down a do-nothing budget that triggered a crisis of confidence among foreign financiers in the Canadian dollar. If Canada's political culture does not change, its policies are bringing about the break-up as well as the economic collapse of the country.

Despite such dire possibilities, arrogance has characterized Canada's political scene. There are many examples. There is rampant patronage and pork-barrelling. There was Pierre Elliott Trudeau's refusal to impeach, or even criminally charge, Liberal Francis Fox even after he admitted that he had forged the signature of his lover's husband to facilitate her abortion. Likewise, Ontario's New Democrats refused to kick out of the legislature a former Tourism minister who was accused of propositioning a woman in a bar by promising her a government job in return for sexual favours. No less shabby was the fact that Tory MP Jean Charest was removed temporarily from cabinet by Prime Minister Brian Mulroney, only to be reinstated a short while later, even though Charest had called a judge in an attempt to influence a court decision. The list of arrogant and illegal acts involving persons from all political parties goes on and on and on.

Canada has been captive to a generation of politicians who have ignored polls showing that the majority of Canadians want capital punishment, tougher consequences for young offenders, and, recently, an end to the country's current level, and type, of immigration. As if to thumb its nose at Canadians, Ottawa's bureaucracy even tried to prevent the extradition to the United States of the fugitive Charles Ng, who stood accused of a series of heinous murders in the United States. The bureaucratic intervention was based on the possibility that Ng's extradition to California might result in his execution. The rationale given was that no accused person in Canada should face a penalty disallowed by Canadian law, and Canada does not permit capital punishment. Not only was this defence offensive in itself, and a waste of time and taxpayers' money, it also raised the possibility that an alleged murderer would have been set loose in Canada.

We might have had a united country led by politicians who responded to the needs and wishes of the majority. Instead we have had a generation of politicians who have divided us by pandering to minorities. Unable at times to reconcile what the majority in English Canada wanted with what the majority in French Canada wanted, federal politicians in Canada opted for consensus among themselves to establish the legitimacy of their actions. The assumption that an élite can make decisions among themselves, without reference to the majority of citizens, is invalid and cannot be sustained. Canadians want change.

STATE-SUPPORTED OPPRESSION

Freedom has been defined as the right to swing your arm but not hit anyone with it. Swinging your arm is the basis of individual rights. Not allowing one individual to hit another is the principal justification behind the existence of governments. Unfortunately, in Canada, the state has strayed seriously away from this responsibility. We live in a country where individuals are regularly being hit by swinging arms, including government arms. Canada fosters politically sponsored discrimination, unnecessary state intervention, and reductions in everything from freedom of speech to freedom of the press and the rule of law. Canadians do not live in a dictatorship, but we live in an increasingly oppressive country.

By ignoring the birthrights and freedoms of Canadians, the country's politicians are playing with fire. Successful Canadians, like successful citizens everywhere, no longer put up with tax systems, political systems, or economic systems they do not respect or cannot succeed in. Refusing to be shackled to a jurisdiction they despise, or that they believe is out to destroy them, they take themselves and their capital elsewhere. This is the new reality of the next century: the empowerment of the individual thanks to free trade, global access and the information highway. And Canada — unless it reconstitutes itself — is falling victim to massive tax-evasion, -avoidance, and exile strategies.

At the moment, the flow of people and money out of the country, while increasing, is hardly a torrent. But should the richest — and therefore most mobile — Canadians suddenly decide to leave en masse, they would abandon the vast majority of Canadians who are handcuffed to the country as employees. These are the real victims of bad governance, not the wealthy who can escape or hide.

Unions are just one of the examples of the proclivity in this country for governments to encroach on our freedom to communicate, read, and speak. But there are many laws and restrictions which, in aggregate, are equally damaging to individual rights. Billed as "employment equity" or "fair employment" policies, these are simply reverse discrimination and should be illegal.

As a feminist, I am outraged by employment equity rules that would force employers to hire a quota of women at pay that is identical to men's. That's appropriate if they do exactly the same job, but my experience has been that women, quite often, are considerably less valuable as workers than males are. For instance, a radio news editor polled his reporters, male and female, to see who was willing to work through the holidays. His three male reporters volunteered to do overtime and any shift. His three female workers balked. This is not unusual, nor is it unusual for a firm to lose a female to maternity leave for as much as nine months.

Another example involved a law firm whose female partners were creating an issue out of the fact that none was a senior partner. "But none of them was willing to drop everything at a moment's notice and fly somewhere or other for a client," said a friend at the firm. "This was because of family considerations or other matters."

The point is, there's nothing wrong with a value system that places relationships above making money. But women cannot have it both ways, and public policy should not let them. Feminism is about fairness and equality because women have been treated as second-class citizens. It's not about revenge or imagined male conspiracies or reducing men to second-class citizens.

Society's goal should be to create a meritocracy. Those who work smartest and hardest deserve to earn the most. That's not to say that a meritocracy exists now. Men routinely hire fraternity brothers, drinking buddies, or squash partners, often shutting out women or other outsiders. But businesses cannot carry incompetent staff for long, and eventually those who do not deserve their jobs will lose them. This will increasingly be the case as the world becomes more competitive.

Two employment equity victims that made headlines were Jake Smola and Michael Buckborough of Ontario. Smola applied to become a fire-fighter, and Buckborough to become a cop. "The police force wouldn't even take my application," noted Buckborough, "because I'm a white male."

Smola went public with his complaint when he scored higher on an entrance exam with the City of Kitchener, only to find that a female with lower score got in before him to fill the "female quota." The problem, said the city's mayor in an interview, was that the quotas were imposed on municipalities by the former Liberal government. He was correct. Employment equity was first pushed by Ottawa and passed on down the line through other levels of government. Now the situation is that the public sector is required to have representation from the five "EE" (employment equity) pools — francophones, visible minorities, aboriginals, females, and the disabled.

Sometimes concern about "equality" reaches comic proportions. In 1993, the Ontario government circulated information to its civil servants to lay down rules about appropriate social behaviour between the sexes. One expert used as an example in presentations he gave a case involving a group of five men and two women who work closely together. Every Friday night, he said, the five guys went drinking together at a strip club called the Club Zanzibar. Their two female colleagues complained because they were "excluded" from going by virtue of the fact they were never invited. They grieved to the provincial agency in charge of this silliness and won. The men were called in and given a warning. Each had a black mark, or negative reference to the incident, entered in his personnel record as having been guilty of "poisoning the workplace." The point is, the women were essentially saying that they wanted — and deserved — to be invited to the Zanzibar because they worked with these five men. But if the five had taken them to the Zanzibar that probably would have constituted sexual harassment.

While such incidents are amusing, such intrusions into freedom of speech and expression are extremely worrisome. Canada's tradition in this regard is chequered at best. We have some of the most oppressive libel and slander restrictions in the English-speaking world, which explains, at least in part, the timidity and mediocrity of most of the country's media. The principal problem with libel laws in Canada is the reverse onus. Journalists must show that their published allegations are not libellous. It is not for the accuser to prove his or her accusations. This makes defence against charges of libel extremely difficult and expensive because defendants rather than plaintiffs must mount a case. It is unfair because it is the equivalent of asking a doctor accused of malpractice to disprove the allegations against him. The burden of proof should reside with the accuser.

While the British have similar libel laws, Canada has the dubious distinction of being the only country with a category called "criminal libel" which is a jailable offence. This is a distant legal cousin of Canada's disgraceful "Hate Laws," under which people can be imprisoned for stirring up hatred. These laws impose outrageous limits on freedom of expression, speech, and the press. The despicable Nazi Ernst Zundel was actually jailed for publishing his view that the Holocaust never happened. The irony here is that the same type of restrictions on speech and the press were deployed by Nazi Germany to help facilitate its persecution of the Jews, gypsies, Slavs, and political rivals.

The tolerance in Canada for such laws has probably contributed to the passage of other laws and setting up of commissions that curb individual freedoms. The New Democrats in British Columbia decided in 1994 to set up a Hate Commission made up of political appointees who will investigate and prosecute any person who bad-mouths individuals or groups because of their ethnic or religious background, gender, disability, sexual proclivity, or physical characteristics. This will be a Star Chamber against perceived, imagined, and even proven "bigots." But it is simply one set of bigots watching another.

This is similar to Ontario's Office of the Commission, Harassment and Discrimination, designed to stamp out bigotry in the education system. Chief "H & D" officer is New Democrat Stephen Lewis, whose job is to crack down on verbal harassment or discrimination. This is defined as "one or a series of vexatious comments or conduct related to one or more of the prohibited grounds that is known or might reasonably be known to be unwelcome/unwanted, offensive, intimidating, hostile or inappropriate." Examples include "gestures, remarks, jokes, taunting, innuendo, display of offensive materials, offensive graffiti, threats, verbal or physical assault, imposition of academic penalties, hazing, stalking, shunning or exclusion related to the prohibited grounds."

Perhaps such laws merely reflect the good manners, and the distaste for unseemly controversy, that characterize the average Canadian. But enlisting the law to impose manners on people should be illegal because it can only lead to injustice. These commissions are more than politically motivated Star

Chambers. Along with so-called human-rights commissions, they also represent an erosion of the rule of law or of due process: "Accused" persons are guilty until proven innocent, and proceedings ignore the proper rules of evidence and guarantees to legal representation or to cross-examination. Rulings by these commissions can ruin careers and lives.

Unfortunately, the right of the state to intervene is well established, and Canada's governments keep pushing for even more restrictions. The misuse or mishandling by governments of "freedom of information" or "access to information" laws is a case in point. Canadian governments have never really conceded that the public has a right to know. Officials reserve the right to decide whether to release the documents sought, in whole or in part. In denying access or, when they restrict access, they need not give any reason, nor is there any appeal process by which information can be obtained. And from withholding documents in this way, it is only a short journey to outright censorship.

The most glaring example of government censorship involved Susan Eng, the Toronto lawyer in charge of the city's police commission, who criticized a policeman for disclosing the fact that blacks commit proportionally more crimes than other racial groups. Her ban on disclosing such information amounted to censorship, which was not in the public interest. Similarly, federal immigration officials refused to release to the *Vancouver Sun* some 1993 reports describing the extent of welfare fraud committed by refugees. Federal immigration officials were reluctant in the mid-1980s when I requested a copy of the decision which allowed former Philippines dictator Ferdinand Marcos's notorious sidekick, Dewey Dee, to remain as a refugee in Canada.

All three mainstream parties, as members of an all-party

federal parliamentary committee, combined to pass Bill C-114 — a gag law. The law would imprison for five years any individual or group that independently spent more than $1,000 to support or oppose parties or candidates during elections. The law was struck down as unconstitutional in a court challenge supported by the National Citizens' Coalition on June 25, 1993. The court said the gag law violated our freedoms of speech and association, and our right to an informed vote.

"If the courts uphold Bill C-114, then the day an election is called, only journalists and politicians would be allowed to use the mass media to urge voters to vote for or against candidates," said coalition spokesman David Somerville. "Put another way, this bill would deny non-journalists or non-politicians mass media access during an entire election campaign. That is distinctly unfair in a country where the majority is supposed to rule and not a couple of élites.

"The Ottawa political élites learned nothing from their resounding defeat on the Charlottetown Accord vote. They must understand that Canadians want to be included in the political process, not be shut up and shut out. I believe the real reason for this gag law is that the political establishment wants to force citizens to channel their political spending through the parties, rather than to speak out independently."

The gag-law decision in Alberta was appealed by the federal government, even though it is an embarrassment in a mature democracy.

STATE CONFISCATION

Armed with censorship and other unconstitutional weapons, Canada's governments wreak incalculable damage in the

marketplace. Canadians have no legal or constitutional protection against the seizure of their property, or the arbitrary
diminution of its value by government fiat or action. Back in
1909, Mr. Justice Riddell of the Supreme Court of Ontario
said, "the prohibition 'thou shalt not steal' has no legal force
upon the sovereign body." That remains true today because
property rights are not protected under either the constitution
or the Charter of Rights and Freedoms.

Article 17 of the U.N. Declaration of Human Rights, which
includes clauses protecting property ownership from arbitrary
seizure, was signed by Canada. The North American Free
Trade Agreement also contains protections against state
"theft" (expropriation without compensation) among the
three signatory countries. American and Mexican nationals
cannot have their property taken or diminished in value in
Canada, but Canadians have no such protection, except in
other countries.

Prime Minister John Diefenbaker's government enacted a
Canadian Bill of Rights which included "the right of the individual to life, liberty, security of the person and the enjoyment
of property and the right not to be deprived thereof except by
due process of law." Unfortunately, this has had little or no
effect because it was not enshrined in the constitution or
Charter of Rights, so that it can be overridden by legislation at
any time. No attempt was made to insert property rights in the
constitution. Property rights were opposed by the socialist
New Democrats led by Saskatchewan premier Allan Blakeney;
in order to curry his favour the reference was dropped from
the Charter altogether. Now the charter reads: "Everyone has
the right to life, liberty and security of the person and the right
not to be deprived thereof except in accordance with the principles of fundamental justice."

This is a fundamental flaw in the Canadian nation-state and has done great harm to our capitalist system already.

In the absence of protections, great harm has been done to individuals, through legislation, regulation, or government inaction. For instance, Kenneth Hook of Flinton, Ontario, and Lorne Neyedly of Lockport, Manitoba, are among the thousands of victims of state intervention in the economy which caused them damage, but about which they have no legal remedy against governments. Both pay taxes as pheasant farmers, and they wrote to various Agriculture officials to get Canada to back off a subsidy program that was using their tax dollars to drive them out of business.

Hook said the federal government decided to help struggling farmers diversify and targeted the pheasant market as a particularly lucrative one. In 1990, Ottawa, in cooperation with the Saskatchewan Pheasant Producers Co-Operative, encouraged farmers to get into full-scale pheasant production. Too many followed their advice. The result was predictable: a huge glut of birds developed, prices plummeted, and non-subsidized farmers like Hook and Neyedly are in financial trouble.

"The typical wholesale price of pheasant has been about $4.60 per pound, but the pheasant co-op is offering them at $3 per pound, dumping pheasants across Canada at distress prices," said Hook.

Neyedly wrote Ottawa: "We have managed to become one of Canada's largest exporters of high-quality pheasants to Japan. As well we have built an extensive Canadian distribution network. Competition within our industry is keen but the playing field was level. We have been involved for many years with various federal and provincial government departments involved in putting on seminars and agricultural shows. We have been pleased to assist those interested in developing export and diverse markets in whatever way we can. We did not expect to have the rug pulled from beneath us."

The Saskatchewan co-op was warned that the market was collapsing and shrinking, but this advice was ignored, and governments just threw more tax dollars into the fray. "We hear subsidies are $1.81 per pound, which is what's killing us," Neyedly said. So, at the end of the day, we have government getting in the way of well-established exporters by artificially driving down prices.

These farmers should sue Agriculture Canada for damages, but they can't. Canada's laws protect governments from litigation, even in clear-cut cases of state oppression or unequal treatment. The case of Toronto furrier Paul Magder showed that there is virtually no remedy against punitive or wrong-headed government action. Magder defied Sunday-shopping laws in Ontario for years, arguing that the area where his store was located was exempted from the laws because it was mostly Chinese retailers and deemed to be a tourist area. But the bylaw specifically excluded him from the provisions that allowed his neighbours to stay open. Magder and his lawyer went to the Supreme Court of Canada twice, first on the grounds that the law infringed his religious freedoms, and then on the grounds that the law was discriminatory. He lost the first round on a technicality, and the second because the judges decided that because Sunday shopping had been made legal his case would be dismissed. The court simply abandoned him. The province subsequently upped his fines to $535,000 and demanded immediate payment. This act of governmental meanness pushed Magder from receivership into bankruptcy, a particularly pointless exercise, one would have thought, given that the fines would never be paid and the law had been changed so that Sunday shopping was now allowed.

"He has a case for malicious prosecution, and if we could have a jury I could get him millions in damages for what the government has done to him. But the law prohibits a jury trial when it comes to suing government for damages," said his lawyer, Tim Danson. "And a judge will protect the system."

Magder's case is a cautionary tale. It shows what happens when an individual in this country takes on city hall or a provincial government. But more people should make the attempt, despite the enormous cost in time and money. Another example of a battle worth fighting involved a Toronto developer who sued Ontario's New Democrats for their damaging retroactive rent-control legislation. The law amounts to confiscation without compensation and has ruined the value of all residential rental units in the province. The bill went considerably further than merely controlling rent. It allows tenants to get rent roll-backs or financial compensation if maintenance or fixtures are not to their liking. Worse yet — and the basis of the developer's suit — is that when the bill was brought in, any rent increases exceeding 4 per cent which had been granted but had not taken effect as of that particular time were rescinded. This brought a number of landlords to their knees; they were in default, and foreclosures have been commonplace.

Ontario's day-care operators have also been hurt by government intervention which has damaged them. Their association submitted a brief in 1993 which documented the damage wreaked on their businesses by government edict.

"The recession resulted in fewer child-care spaces being utilized in the past two years and independents or non-profits alike have closed," it said. But the province kept building more day-care centres. The government's central planners also ignored the shifting demographics, the declining birth rate and the fact that 90 per cent of households will never need day care. The result was many business bankruptcies or others closing their doors before the inevitable. Not surprisingly, many private day-care operators either closed their doors or declared bankruptcy. One day-care operator bulldozed his centre after he had decided to call it quits. He called television cameras onto the scene so they could capture on film his message to Ontario's New Democrats, which was that they may have stolen his business but they weren't going to get his building.

There are few recent examples of government confiscation as huge or hugely unfair as British Columbia's expropriation in 1993 of hundreds of thousands of hectares of land to make a provincial park. Peggy Witte, owner of Royal Oak Resources Ltd., had a 42 per cent stake in an ore body found amidst the proposed parkland which had a potential to produce $550 million worth of minerals. It was perhaps coincidental that Witte's company is hated by B.C.'s union masters. Her company hired replacement workers at its Yukon mine, and police have charged several union workers with the murder of eight of those replacements. Perhaps the park was a way to settle old scores. Fortunately, she's suing for compensation.

Of course, confiscation is nothing new to Canadian governments. The hated National Energy Policy included provisions to seize offshore lands from foreign-owned multinationals. The Parti Québécois nationalized the asbestos industry with a take-it-or-leave-it price, among other businesses, and New Democrats in Saskatchewan and Manitoba seized mines, forests, and other enterprises. There's also the problem of crown corporations which compete unfairly against private-sector rivals whose taxes are used to lose them business. Everything from the CBC to Air Canada, Petro-Canada, and dozens of others have restricted the ability of Canadians to survive economically.

SOCIAL APARTHEID

Perhaps one of the root causes of Canada's "group rights" mentality has to do with the fact that we separate our children at the age five along religious and linguistic lines. The existence of more than one tax-supported school system has, in my opinion, contributed greatly toward dividing the country linguistically and in other ways. The acceptance of educational apartheid probably led to multiculturalism, a policy that has spawned an industry and done more harm to building consensus or a national identity than any other policy. Multiculturalism is also a serious deviation from the concept of a liberal, pluralistic society where individuals have rights. Now groups are more important than individuals.

"The single biggest problem is that this country has a charter of rights and freedoms that is unable to distinguish between collectivities and rights of the individual," said C.D. Howe Institute chief Tom Kierans. "English Canada is prepared to become more Americanized, with individual rights predominant, while that is not the case in French Canada, where the equilibrium point [between individual and group rights] is different. But the law of the land states that group rights outweigh the good of the individual, and that's just not acceptable to many Canadians."

Similarly, Robert Fulford wrote about the problem of multiculturalism in March 1994 after the Writers' Union of Canada newsletter announced a Racial Minority Writers Committee conference for 150 participants. The catch was that only First Nations writers and writers of colour were invited, even though the government was helping to finance the event. "The old liberal pluralism holds each of us has rights as an individual — an idea that propelled social progress for generations. The new multiculturalism focuses on the rights of groups and sees each of us as a member of a racially designated cluster. Pluralism maintains individuals should be seen as unique persons, race is secondary. Multiculturalism is that people should be first seen as members of a group. Pluralism is color blind. Multiculturalism isn't," wrote Fulford.

Another equality issue which Canada must sort out involves its First Nations, or aboriginal, people. As debt problems bear down more and more heavily on Canadians, the issue of fairness in taxation will arise. And, for a variety of historical and other reasons, aboriginals in Canada enjoy enormous entitlements including not having to pay any taxes. To boot, their demands know few bounds for the future. Land claims in British Columbia are equivalent to 130 per cent of the province's entire land mass. And governments oblige readily, tying future taxpayers to enormous obligations.

In the early 1990s, the federal government set up the eastern Inuit "nation" of Nunavut. Its 18,000 people will share $1.15 billion over fourteen years, or $63,888 each. They also gain the royalties and spin-off benefits from whatever mineral wealth is discovered there in future, and despite such assets and cash, Canadian taxpayers are also subsidizing 80 per cent of the cost of the existing territorial government. More money will be spent setting up Inuit self-government, training programs, and other entitlements already in place, such as free housing and fuel. Canada is building a vast, perpetual welfare state north of its 60th parallel and on reservations for one million aboriginals who pay no taxes. Tax-free reserve businesses compete unfairly against off-reserve enterprises. Worse yet, aboriginal lands are exempt from the rule of law, so that everything from smuggling to casinos, to wife-beating, is not subjected to Canadian law and order.

THE ABUSE OF QUEBEC'S ANGLOPHONES

In the desperation by Ottawa and Quebec-born prime ministers to stave off separation, Canadian politicians have totally abandoned anglophone Quebeckers. Even so-called federalist Prime Minister Jean Chrétien showed his extraordinarily cavalier attitude toward the rights of his principal supporters in Quebec. "Jean Chrétien said to a Sault Ste. Marie audience on October 10, 1993 that anglophones are completely at home in Quebec. He made this statement knowing that anglophones in Quebec have their rights and their language restricted by provincial legislation, that English immigrants cannot send their children to English schools and that some 200,000 anglophones [the Equality Party estimates 400,000] have already fled the province. His statement demonstrated the continuing facade used by federal politicians that allows them to ignore the racism against English-speaking Canadians in Quebec and the violations of fundamental rights contained in the Quebec French Language charter," wrote Maurice King, a Quebec municipal politician in 1993.

The language battles demonstrate the disregard for minorities, or for children, by the separatist élite. Quebec's racist charter was found to have transgressed the 1962 U.N. Covenant on Economic, Social and Cultural Rights. A section of the covenant stated that "primary education shall be available free to all," and another stipulates that all rights must be "exercised without discrimination of any kind as to race, color, sex, language, national or social origin, birth, or other status."

Despite the U.N. declaration, the Parti Québécois adopted a charter in 1977 which severely restricted access to English-language schools, proscribing from attendance the children of francophones and immigrants. In the intervening years, the population of students in English-language schools has shrunk to 100,000 from 250,000, a 60 per cent reduction. Hundreds of English schools closed. By 1993, there were more French-language schools in Ontario for its tiny French minority — less than 10 per cent of the population — than there were English-language schools in Quebec, with 30 per cent of its population anglophone or immigrant. In 1991, 89 per cent of anglophones polled in Quebec disagreed with the fact that French was the only language of instruction for immigrant children, but their provincial party of choice — the Liberals — did nothing.

"In the last two decades English-speaking Canadians in Quebec have seen their fundamental human rights and the rule of law sacrificed in the politically expedient attempt to appease French Canadian nationalism," said Equality Party head Keith Henderson.

Trudeau's constitution also discriminated against English. Section 23(1)(a) of the Canadian constitution confers the right to send a child to an English or French school across Canada. But section 59(1) gives Quebec permission to decide whether it will provide access to English or not. The bottom line is that the constitution gives a French immigrant to

Toronto the right to send his or her child to a French school. But a British or American immigrant to Montreal would have no right to send his or her child to an English school.

A 1993 U.S. State Department Human Rights Report had this to say about Canada: "Rights are generally respected in practice, but Canada's multicultural society continues to experience some problems of discrimination. Non-French speakers in Quebec continued to face difficulties in 1993. Law 86, amending the language law in 1993, did not broaden access to English-language schooling. The province argues that the education and sign laws protect French language and culture, but those who prefer English resent these restrictions. Because of the atmosphere engendered by the language laws and a perceived lack of economic opportunity in Quebec for those whose mother tongue is not French, many young English-speakers born there have left the province."

It's little wonder they leave. They are the victims of revisionism and repression. Even the CBC refused to air a fascinating and accurate National Film Board documentary by William Weintraub about the discrimination against Quebec's English-speaking minority since the mid-1970s.

The struggle by the anglophones to get the rights afforded to Canadians outside their province has led to an exodus and given Canada a very black eye. A May 1993 decision by a committee of the United Nations ruled that Canada's sign bylaw abrogated human rights in Quebec. The request to the committee was made by Gordon McIntyre in 1988 after getting notice from provincial authorities that he had to take down an English sign. He was a victim of hate calls and threats and was ridiculed in the press and called a racist.

Less high profile, but more harmful, is the fact that

anglophone Quebeckers have been excluded from the public-sector pie — in the form of jobs or services — that the majority divide among themselves.

King wrote that the province's nurses in the 1990s had to pass tough French-language examinations. The immigrant, or those who couldn't speak French, nurses were forced to leave because they couldn't pass the tests. In May 1993, Dr. Harry Polansky, a dentist, actually charged officials at Ste. Anne's Veterans' Hospital with using the Quebec charter for linguistic cleansing in staffing the hospital: "Anglophone nurses are failed in French oral exams while francophone nurses with an indifferent ability in English are regularly given passing grades in the English oral exam."

The province is also encroaching on an anglophone's right to have his day in court. In the 1993 fall session, Casper Bloom, *batonnier* of the Bar of Montreal, drew attention to the serious erosion of the right to use English in law. He lamented the loss of Montreal's image as "being an open, tolerant, thriving, cosmopolitan centre with two major languages in use."

Bloom said the Barreau du Québec, which serves all members, including 2,000 anglophone lawyers, operates exclusively in French, and there is not one anglophone among its staff of 140 people. He said that out of 1,000 people employed at the Palais de Justice, there are only 3 or 4 anglos. All reports and notices are in French, and even if proceedings are in English, judgments are routinely rendered in French. These discriminatory practices have resulted in a growing reluctance on the part of lawyers to use English in court, lest officials be offended, even if the accused speaks only English.

The excuse commonly used for such behaviour is that the

very survival of the French culture is at stake. Francophones believe that bilingualism results in a shift to English, which is why they must ram French down everyone's throats. They also feel that they are still disadvantaged and need affirmative action programs. King wrote that these are fallacies, and that after twenty years of mistreatment of anglos, francophones now control 62 per cent of all Quebec companies, up from 47 per cent in 1961. He also pointed out that 80 per cent of managerial jobs are held by francophones who are also vastly overrepresented in Ottawa. Lastly, for thirty of the last forty-two years, Canada's prime minister has been from Quebec. In other words, if Quebec's francophones are disadvantaged, it must be their own fault.

What's really involved here is bullying and revenge for perceived wrongs in the past. Doug Fullerton, in his book *Dangerous Delusion*, wrote: "the French language charter is a regressive document more concerned with righting past wrongs to French Canadians and curtailing the use of English than with pursuing the entirely proper goal of encouraging a greater use of the French language in Quebec. There is a whiff of the Prussian jackboot about it, an aura of coercion, racism, revenge."

Canada's democracy and capitalism have been badly bruised as a result of state intervention. The tendency to ride roughshod over rights considered inviolate in the United States or United Kingdom has discouraged many Canadian entrepreneurs and voters alike. The polite tolerance for state interference has led to a body of laws, rules, and commissions that infringe on the freedoms that Canadians have a right to enjoy. They also are a constant irritant to most people and have led to disenchantment with the country itself.

These arrogant institutions and laws have led to bad governance, contributing in some measure toward the fact that successive regimes have been able to ring up a hideous debt that threatens the nation's very existence. Fixing the debt, and lowering taxes, will attack only the symptoms. Canada must restrict the role of the state permanently, and return to its roots as a liberal pluralistic democracy.

WHERE DO WE
GO FROM HERE?

S THE TWENTY-FIRST CENTURY APPROACHES, CANADA will continue to suffer from an exodus of individuals, businesses, capital, and spirit until it solves its intrinsic problems. The cause is a succession of governments that have so mismanaged our affairs that Canada is now afflicted with a cancerous debt; oversized governments; a large and growing underground economy; a virulent and damaging Quebec separatist movement; Western alienation; extreme dependency on the state by the underclass, the Maritime provinces, and aboriginals; and laws which impose union and other varieties of oppression.

And yet, many Canadians do not understand what awaits them if tough reforms are not introduced. Canadian governments have been allowed to borrow increasing amounts of money to make the interest payments on their debts, with the result that the actual cost of overspending is never reflected in our taxes, but is simply piled on top of other accumulated debts. Eventually, the burden will become too heavy, and the cost of carrying the debt impossible. This will certainly happen by the turn of the century.

Meanwhile, the country's political élite occupy a rarefied realm far away from ordinary Canadians who increasingly find themselves as if underground — trying to escape the onerous and interventionist policies of the people who rule them. This situation cannot last. Chances are, neither will Canada.

As things stand, Canada probably has only three choices. It can drift along as the "Scotland" of North America, a hinterland with its own Parliament but increasingly dependent on its southern neighbour. It can become a well-managed, diverse confederation like Switzerland, exploiting competitive advantages and niche markets. Or it can become part of the United States. These are the choices, with or without Quebec, and it all depends on how we play our economic cards. But play is not going well.

The third option, amalgamation with the United States, is almost certain to occur by the turn of the century unless the country dramatically restructures and comes to grips with government overspending. Some Canadians may welcome union, but I happen to think it would be unfortunate. It's one thing to enjoy a visit to the United States. It's quite another to put up with its crime rates and social problems. As a former American who has lived in Canada since 1966, I believe Canada should do everything in its power to maintain its sovereignty.

Union may be avoided precisely by the sort of cataclysmic events that are looming on Canada's wide horizon. A secession threat by Quebec or a full-blown debt crisis could lead to necessary reform. But this will happen only if strong leaders emerge who know what needs doing and who can convince Canadians to make sacrifices. Of course, crises could also have the opposite effect, precipitating more problems and speeding Canada on the way to statehood.

"It's not a matter of if Canada becomes part of the States, but when," said Jimmy Pattison. "Everything is north–south. Taxes in Canada are just awful, and deficits are worse. Eighty per cent of my executives want to be transferred to the U.S. The underground economy is huge. That's the real world. It's not a case of disloyalty. Canadians are not leaving their country. Their country has left them."

Others agree. "Canada is doomed. I think it is hopeless," said Victor Rice, the CEO who moved the former Massey-Ferguson Limited, now called Varity Corporation, to the United States for tax, and other, reasons in 1991. "Canada cannot afford its medical system. It's too close to the border to have all those expensive layers of government. Just look at the situation. What competitive advantages does Canada have? Resources? I think the value of resources will decline by 40 per cent over the next ten years because of environmental constraints. Canada's other competitive advantage was low electricity costs, but that advantage is now gone too."

Rice agrees that the only out is the Swiss model. "Canada has only one choice. It is sleeping next to a giant, and its biggest opportunity — perhaps gone for good — is to become a tax haven. It once was, in the 1960s. Now it may be too late. I lived seventeen years in Canada and I learned that Canadian nationalism is nothing more than anti-Americanism, and you can't build a national pride or a nation on negatives like that."

The debt situation is frightening and may have reached the point of no return, according to Tom Kierans, head of the economic think-tank the C.D. Howe Institute in Toronto. "The situation in Canada is very, very dangerous, and we have a totally intractable debt problem. My fear is that governments will suddenly have to take a meat-axe and, our kinder, gentler society will be changed without intelligently doing it. We must retain dignity for our citizens while maintaining incentives to work. But when the axe falls hard on Canadians, the question becomes: so what's the difference between Canada and the U.S.? What that leads to is the dissipation of the will to sustain the country."

There is no guarantee, of course, that union with the United States is easily available to Canada. The United States does not, in my opinion, covet Canada, with its Quebec, aboriginal, and debt problems. But Washington would be in a position to dictate terms and absorb Canada's governmental debts without much indigestion. Acquiring Canada would cost perhaps $1 trillion, or roughly in today's dollars what Washington wasted in Vietnam. But unlike that dreadful misadventure, the absorption of Canada would mean securing its biggest border forever and creating the biggest, most resource-rich country on earth. To boot, the United States would "acquire" 27 million educated and enterprising citizens.

The United States could take over Canada in the same way West Germany "took over" East Germany. The U.S. Treasury would simply swap Canadian for American dollars one-for-one. Canada could either negotiate statehood status, or become a "commonwealth" of America like Puerto Rico.

Former Liberal cabinet minister Donald MacDonald may be one of the few hold-outs who still thinks Canadian sovereignty is secure. "I think the debt can be managed. It took a long time to get into debt and it'll take time to get out of it. As for becoming part of the U.S., we've become a major player with our own identity. There's a will to keep together. We don't want decisions made for us. We want to run our own show."

NO STATUS QUO

He is right, of course: it is still possible for us to sort out our mess as other countries in similarly dire straits have done. But, for a number of reasons, Canada may be one of the world's most vulnerable nations. Such measures as Draconian exchange controls, higher taxes, and deficit-cutting measures which dramatically reduce living standards simply won't do the trick because Canadians have options open to them that the citizens of almost no other nation possess.

Some 50 per cent of Canadians probably have access to another passport. Theoretically, all Canadians have access to the United States through the green card or visa process, or illegal migration. What all these options mean is that Canadians can leave if the going gets tough. Most likely to leave are those immigrants who already had the gumption to leave other countries to settle in Canada. About one in six Canadians is an immigrant, according to the 1991 census. Others who are inclined to move will find that the citizenship rules in other countries offer various opportunities for them.

Two in six Canadians have British ancestry, for example, and most of these, if not all, have at least one British-born grandparent, which means they are entitled to full European Union citizenship, complete with medical benefits. Canadians also have the option of living in the dozens of commonwealth countries. Another half-million or so already do. Millions more come from countries where citizenship rules have been liberalized. The United States, Ireland, Italy, Israel, for instance, now allow dual nationality. The United States extends citizenship to children with one American parent, even if that child is born in Canada or elsewhere. Under the North American Free Trade Agreement, Canadians can more easily emigrate to the prosperous United States than ever before. Historically, Canadians have been the third-largest group to immigrate to the United States, and there's every reason to think the trend will continue. While wholesale migration may not be in the cards for most Canadians, the most productive and entrepreneurial individuals certainly won't put up with the huge pain and sacrifices which may be necessary to preserve the country. They are already leaving — or their capital is.

Currently, an incredible 3 million Canadians "live" in the United States either permanently or part-time — more than 10 per cent of the population of Canada. This represents an enormous erosion of commitment. Even more significant, this 10 per cent probably represents Canada's most entrepreneurial, adaptable, and wealthiest citizens. Even those who only maintain vacation homes in the United States are well heeled and may control directly and indirectly a huge proportion of Canada's GDP.

Those who think that the disappearance of Canada is unlikely should be aware that, in fact, nations disappear all the time. Newfoundland racked up unmanageable debts during the Great Depression. After being propped up by Britain through the war, its citizens opted in 1949 to become part of Canada. Canadians, like Newfoundlanders, are headed toward an unmanageable debt and may opt to join our gigantic neighbour to the south rather than undergo the slow and painful process of regaining fiscal responsibility.

"It's actually rare in North America for little mini-nations to exist, and we've had them give up throughout history," said University of Toronto historian Michael Bliss. "Most tellingly, Newfoundland was a case of an independent country saying 'We can't face the debt.' Yes, Canada is also in danger. The cancer eating at the heart of this country is the debt. Not Quebec."

Bliss pointed out that debts also led British Columbia to join Confederation in 1871, after Britain became sick of supporting it. Two years later, Prince Edward Islanders joined Canada, after building a railway they couldn't afford. In essence, the country was stitched together out of bankruptcies: three out of the ten provinces had no choice but to join. Then Canada itself nearly went under building the east–west railway.

An increasing number of observers, like Toronto investment banker Andrew Sarlos, think Canadians shouldn't bother to fight against the inevitable end. Sarlos, himself, came to Canada in 1956 as a refugee from the Soviet invasion of Hungary. "Canada should become part of the United States," he said. "Ask yourself. I was willing to die for independence for Hungary in 1956, but I'm not willing to die to keep Canada from becoming part of the United States. Neither would my son be willing to die. There is very little to distinguish Canada from the United States now, and Canadians won't sacrifice their living standards to avoid a merger because there's no reason to do so.

"We are not even pretending any more to have an armed force to defend Canada. If a country relies 100 per cent on the U.S. to defend itself, what right has that country to call itself an independent nation? Austria and Switzerland have larger armed forces than Canada does. If you ask Canadians in a poll would they want to be part of the U.S., the answer would be no," he said. "But when asked if they would be willing to give up 5 per cent of their standard of living to maintain a military force or to restore tariff barriers, the answer is no."

Economic and social policy "with the exception of health care at the moment" are also identical, Sarlos pointed out. "I'm proud to be Canadian and I love this country. I came as a homeless refugee, and getting my Canadian passport was the biggest thing in my life. But the minute you don't spend money to defend your borders or maintain your military because your deficit is too high, you have sold your sovereignty," he said. "It's too late to become a Switzerland because I don't believe Canadians will make the sacrifices necessary."

Michael Bliss doesn't think Canada will break up or join the United States, but he admits that, the way things are going, the younger generation may give up. "I would dismiss statehood as the ultimate fall-back position. I do not favour it now. But I'm reasonably comfortable. Canada has been good to me, but not necessarily to my kids. They are going to ask 'What's the cost of being Canadian?' What's the break point as the costs rise? We have an uncontrollable debt and higher taxes and far fewer services. That is the price we must pay unless you get Ralph Klein types in Ottawa. But Klein types will create so much pressure it will be hard to hold the country together because of the anger."

Already, the true cost of nationhood may be too dear. Price Waterhouse Ltd. senior tax partner Robert Dart made the calculations. To balance budgets, personal income tax rates would have to go up to 34 per cent from 29 per cent on the first $29,000 of taxable income, to 52 per cent from 42 per cent on $29,000–$57,000, to 66 per cent from 53 per cent on income beyond $73,000; plus GST would have to be 9 per cent, not 7 per cent; and provincial sales taxes would have to increase by 2 per cent each. Import duties and taxes on capital, payrolls, gasoline, tobacco, booze, and luxuries would have to jump by 25 per cent across the board, and corporate income taxes would have to hit 55 per cent, from 44 per cent, for large companies, and 28 per cent, from 22 per cent, for small businesses. By contrast, the U.S. corporate tax rates are between 35 and 40 per cent, Britain's 33 per cent, and most European countries' 40 per cent.

Such tax hikes would force more businesses to leave Canada and spark an even greater brain drain than has already occurred. Besides, higher tax rates would not do the trick because they result in diminishing returns as people leave, evade taxes, or embark on aggressive tax-avoidance strategies, thus reducing tax takes for governments. This is already underway in Canada, and the reason why successive Finance ministers routinely miscalculate their deficits year after year. Higher taxes are counterproductive.

Deficits must be eliminated by cost cutting and massive privatization. Both are a political problem because Canadians have become a nation of deficit dependants. Collective federal-provincial deficits in 1994–95 will be at least $65 billion, or nearly 10 per cent of the economy. To reduce deficits to zero overnight would shrink the economy by 10 per cent, require mass lay-offs of government workers, and cause a recession. The result would be an increase, not a decrease, in government spending because the unemployed civil servants would tap into unemployment insurance. The unemployed civil servants would not pay many taxes, nor would they buy automobiles, televisions, clothes, or houses.

But Canada must gradually wean itself — no matter what the cost. Governments buy trucks, computers, paper clips; civil servants buy houses, tapedecks, and cars: cut-backs will hurt their private-sector suppliers. But Canada is like a teenager with ten credit cards. He can live for years a life based on income he does not generate, but, one day, the card companies will cut him off and the toys he acquired will have to go back to the store.

Canada's debt "crisis" may never arrive, says Tom Kierans. "We won't hit the wall, as Mexico or Argentina did, but we will slowly die of the fiscal equivalent of pernicious anemia. Not a bad way to go. You just lose energy and there's no sudden pain. But in the end you no longer exist."

Canada's "pernicious anemia" continues to creep toward the inevitable as the country's wealth creators give up and leave, as have Magna Inc.'s Frank Stronach, Laidlaw Inc.'s Michael DeGroote, and media tycoon Conrad Black. They, and countless others, now conduct their global affairs from countries like Britain and Switzerland, where governments have been able to provide social safety nets better than Canada's at tax rates considerably lower than ours.

Others who cannot leave permanently, or who refuse to become tax exiles, are becoming tax cheats or tax avoiders. Already, there are indications that Canada's underground-economy has reached Italian proportions. These weaknesses point to the greatest weakness of all: Parliaments in this country are increasingly losing their only legitimacy — the power of the purse — when it comes to fleet-footed, ruthless, or mobile Canadians.

"The young kids cannot do well in Canada any longer, and we're going to be losing them," said Tom Kierans. "I have two daughters, and one's in L.A., an entrepreneur, and I'm not sure she's ever coming back. The other is a painter, in graduate school in the U.S., and wants to be a curator. But here, with the public-sector unions having a lock on everything, no one can get any curatorships, so she may never come back either."

GROWTH WON'T HELP

Another impediment to change is the myth that Canada's debts can be supported indefinitely because of the country's incredible treasure trove of resources. But, during the 1970s, the population and its entitlements began to exceed the revenue from resources. Worse than that, politicians began to devalue the resource base by imposing huge royalties or other taxes, environmental constraints, and misguided industrial strategies. The myth persists and is the reason why two generations of Canadian politicians have overspent. The same myth — particularly the belief that a resource-based megaproject can solve all ills — is also behind the chimera of Quebec sovereignty.

"Historically, this optimism stems from the optimism after the Second World War," said Bliss. "There have always been two conflicting images of Canada — that it is a frozen wasteland or that it is a cornucopia of resource wealth. And the generation that grew up in the 1950s and 1960s — the generation that is still governing Canada today — felt Canada was the northern treasure house. I remember in the 1970s hearing business people sitting around at BNCI [the Business Council on National Issues] saying our resource wealth will carry us through."

The value of our resources is being diminished by government edicts and taxes. Even worse are the confiscatory actions, such as the appropriation by B.C.'s New Democrats in 1993 of a vast area called Windy Craggy for a massive park. Some mining experts maintained that there could be several significant gold ore bodies in Windy Craggy, in addition to the one already discovered, which together would have generated billions of dollars in jobs and economic activity. The B.C. government claimed, erroneously, that the only cost of making a park that few will ever visit was the $80 million spent to find the one mine that is known about.

Every time an excessive royalty or tax is imposed, more red tape is added, and more environmental rules invented, Canada loses its biggest competitive advantage — its natural resources. Like it or not, Canada's standard of living is based mostly on its ability to cut down trees, mine metals and minerals, and produce oil and natural gas. It's also based on making car parts and assembling vehicles for foreigners at lower wages than unionized American autoworkers earn. This is how Canada pay its way in the world. The rest of us — whether we produce newspapers, clothing, or dry-cleaning services — live off these 100 or so wealth creators. We ignore their needs at our own peril.

The Liberals first introduced Canada's huge social spending programs in the 1970s at a time when the commodity cycle worldwide was riding high, thanks mostly to the oil cartel. But oil and other prices cratered, leaving the country in a debt mess similar to, but not as serious, as Mexico's.

The same careless mentality was still obvious in February 1980, when Ottawa's new Liberal government decided to hitch its fiscal fortunes to oil prices, as had the Mexicans and the Arabs. On October 28, 1980, the Liberals introduced their ill-fated National Energy Program — a massive tax grab shrouded in economic nationalism. The espoused goal was to increase Canadian ownership of oil companies, but the hidden benefit was that its new taxes on oil and gas would raise enough money to balance the budget by 1986. Unfortunately, the only way this could come about was if oil prices continued to rise, hitting US$70 a barrel by 1986. As it turned out, Ottawa was no better at calculating future oil prices than was the oil cartel itself. Oil collapsed in 1986, to US$18 from US$36 a barrel. The failed Liberal gamble resulted in disastrous deficits; the alienation of the West; a worse recession than others experienced; and the waste of tens of billions of dollars spent exploring for oil in the Arctic, which is now considered, by those same Liberals, to be too sensitive environmentally to be exploited.

Unable to reform without a crisis, but forced to because of our unique vulnerabilities, Canada faces a grim decade ahead. But eventually, if the country is to survive in whole or in pieces, its leaders must adopt the twenty-first-century paradigm: countries, like companies, must treat their "consumers" as though they were valued customers, not plunder them as though they were mere assets. The myth that Canada's resources can support our social programs, or that Canadians will pay an extra price for them, must be laid to rest once and for all. Then Canada must ruthlessly restructure itself. If it does not, it will likely become North America's next Newfoundland.

SOLVING THE PROBLEM

Canada's debt is a symptom of the mediocre political leadership that has held power in this country since Pierre Elliott Trudeau was elected. Voter apathy has contributed to this condition. So has the fact that Canadians have almost no protection from their governments, politically, culturally, or economically. Canadian governments can behave as if the wishes of the electorate were irrelevant. They are not held accountable through a system of day-by-day checks and balances. Nor does the Charter of Rights and Freedoms provide a countervailing force to government oppression. In fact, ironically, this country's charter does not even provide the protections found in a number of international treaties and protocols that our own federal government has signed. Canadians themselves have lost full protection for their linguistic, workplace, speech, expression, and property rights.

Even more worrisome, Canadians in certain circumstances have lost the right to a fair trial, or remedies against their government's damaging actions. Institutions such as "human rights commissions," "hate commissions," and "labour boards" should be illegal because they operate without appeal, without proper evidence gathering, without the presumption of innocence, and without the right to counsel or a proper cross-examination.

The country's failure to protect its citizens has spawned government abuse. It has also drawn support from large trade labour unions, interventionist politicians such as the Liberals, anti-enterprise socialists, and, most significantly, the nationalist-socialist Parti Québécois. These special-interest groups, in turn, have spawned hundreds of lobbyists and other special-interest groups, which have also combined to undermine consensus and society.

For a generation, separatists have been able to sabotage any efforts to revise the constitution. Socialists, supported by wealthy unions, have set about to sabotage any efforts to curb union powers or to protect property rights in the interests of capitalism. And governments have dabbled in crown corporations or megaprojects and other economic misadventures, which have damaged enterprises by ordinary citizens.

Tragically for the country, there is virtually no way to create a counterbalance to these forces by enshrining the missing individual rights into our constitution or charter. It appears that the country's constitutional amending formula is virtually inoperable. Three attempts to make changes have failed since 1982, and each and every time there is another failed attempt, the country becomes more divided and weakened.

In the absence of sweeping constitutional reform, the country must first address its two immediate threats — Quebec and the debt.

DEALING WITH THE QUEBEC HEADACHE

Parti Québécois leader Jacques Parizeau does not represent a grass-roots movement by francophones for self-determination. That is a sham, and Parizeau's actions prove it. What we really have here is the political equivalent of a corporate predator who has failed for thirty years to make an unfriendly takeover. Parizeau's is just what it was thirty years ago: the shareholders are still not willing to give up their assets. Proof of this is Parizeau's flip-flopping in 1994. First he stated that he would consider victory in the next provincial election to be a mandate to secede, following which he would declare his intention to leave and negotiate a deal with the rest of Canada if possible. A separate referendum months later would merely bless the new constitution and terms of exit. Polls must have told Parizeau that he would lose his lead if he made the next election a secession election. So, like any astute takeover artist, Parizeau changed tactics and announced there would be a separate referendum on secession eight to ten months after the election. This is not the behaviour of a man leading a people toward the fulfilment of their overwhelming desires. This is the strategy of a corporate raider biding his time in order to hoodwink shareholders.

Unfortunately, the uncertainty caused by Parizeau's tiresome, time-consuming takeover attempts has eroded the value of the assets owned by all Canadians. Quebec's perennial state of constitutional limbo has cost jobs and a mass exodus of companies, capital, and people over the years. Now you could fire a cannon on many of Montreal's once-vibrant downtown streets without endangering a soul.

Unable to win the hearts and minds of Canadians in Quebec, Parizeau and Bloc Québécois leader Lucien Bouchard embarked in 1994 on a new strategy. Parizeau's job has been to capture Quebec. Bouchard's job has been to woo, or annoy, the other set of "shareholders" who must be manipulated to finish the acquisition — those of us living outside the province. And he's doing a good job of it. He has made himself a lightning-rod to attract abuse from rednecks and direct hostility toward Ottawa with its endless preoccupation with Quebec. He toured western Canada and made himself available on open-line radio shows specifically in order to attract anti-French, anti-Ottawa callers. The idea was to present any hostility as proof of rejection of Quebec and another reason to become independent.

Similarly, Bouchard's cynical decision to assume the office and perquisites of the official opposition leader was designed to agitate, as was his move to Hull and rejection of Stornoway, the opposition leader's official residence. To irritate even more, he has totally neglected his responsibility as opposition leader to represent all Canadian views on national issues. To top it all off, he went to the United States and made outrageous statements about debts and currency. Such manoeuvres, in the absence of support for their cause, have been damaging to every Canadian.

Canada's board of directors — the federal cabinet — must end the takeover attempt. It must ensure that the question of whether Quebeckers want to leave Canada or stay is put bluntly to the electorate on a referendum ballot. The government should then pass legislation forbidding another referendum on this issue for at least twenty years. Such legislation exists in Denmark, Switzerland, and other countries. Ottawa must also make clear that, if Quebec residents opt to launch exit negotiations, Ottawa will hold a referendum among Canadians outside Quebec to see if they approve secession. If negotiations are successful, then two more referendums must be held, one inside and the other outside Quebec, to bless the agreement. The point is that past counter-tactics by Ottawa have failed, and poison pills or scare tactics merely drive away more investment and people. "Greenmail" payments in the form of bribes or special treatment to Quebec are also unacceptable.

The bottom line is the same as with any entity facing a hostile bid: shareholders in the end must believe Canada is worth preserving. So our board of directors must have the courage to let us all affirm this by votes that will bind us together for at least another generation. Then we can all get down to solving the debt problem.

A CHARTER OF RESPONSIBILITIES

To solve the debt and Quebec problems permanently, Canada must redefine the proper role of government. It must ensure that individuals have rights to act as a countervail to government abuse. But at the same time, individuals must also accept responsibilities along with rights. One of the simplest ways to do this would be follow the legislative example set by Switzerland. Canada has a charter of rights. The Swiss have a charter of responsibilities, which, since 1978, has compelled families to look after their needy before governments are asked to intervene. Fathers, mothers, grandparents, and others must support children. Governments in Switzerland sue grandparents on behalf of needy children, and vice versa. The Swiss courts collect the money.

"All persons are bound to contribute towards the maintenance of their ascendants and descendants in the direct line as well as of their brothers and sisters, where without such assistance they would be impoverished," reads the Swiss civil code. "Sisters and brothers can only be made liable to contribute if they themselves are in easy pecuniary circumstances."

If relatives are non-existent or impoverished themselves, the state supports the underprivileged. Where only partial support can be collected, the state tops up the amount until more help can be found. The Swiss have replaced government responsibility wherever possible with individual responsibility. In essence, their social safety net taps relatives first. This ensures the job gets done at considerably less cost to taxpayers.

Meanwhile, in Canada and most other welfare states, governments have let families completely off the hook by forcing taxpayers to support impoverished children or pensioners, directly or indirectly. There were good reasons for this. Governments felt their intervention was necessary because families were breaking up and many family members with the means to do so were unwilling to live up to their responsibilities. Unfortunately, by providing open-ended support, government has compelled taxpaying strangers to meet responsibilities that many families could meet, willingly or otherwise.

What has happened is that we have harnessed tax dollars to lifestyle choices, which simply encourages more people to live off the state. Having a child out of wedlock, for instance, is an extremely expensive lifestyle choice because in our society it compels taxpayers to provide housing and a generous salary to the mother, or whoever is raising the child, for eighteen years. Toronto has 30,000 single parents on assistance; by arithmetical extension, Canada must have around 300,000.

Ontario socialists have gone so far as to allow sixteen-year-olds to get welfare of $612 a month tax-free if they leave home and their parents don't want to support them. The parents do not have to prove they are impoverished.

And all provinces let relatives who have sponsored a loved one as an immigrant off the hook if they say they cannot support him or her any longer. In a region near Toronto, one study showed that 75 per cent of sponsored immigrants were on welfare. Pensioners are yet another problem. In 1991–92, Canadian taxpayers handed out $4.71 billion in special supplements to seniors and their spouses. How many of them have children, grandchildren, or siblings who could afford to contribute something toward their keep? I would guess most, if not all.

Arguments against this system maintain that it is unfair for a grandparent to have to support an unruly, shiftless grandchild who has children out of wedlock. Or unfair for a child to support an aged parent who abused him or her. Or unfair for a rich relative to support all his or her ne'er-do-wells. But those are red herrings. The real unfairness is that governments force the rest of us, who are total strangers, to support those relatives, even when the support isn't needed.

Canadians compelled to provide such supports are angry, and should be. The problem is, politicians either ignore the anger or announce misconceived cuts or crackdowns to tighten up the system. New Brunswick, for instance, wants to pursue fathers for child support and force mothers to cooperate in the pursuit. That's unacceptable. In any event, the father's identity is not always known, even by the mother. The Swiss get around such problems by extending the liability to other relatives. If a mother does not know the father's identity, or does not want his name known, she will force her side of the family to bear his responsibilities. So she has plenty of incentive to get the father to come forward, if only to force his side of the family to contribute to the cause as well.

The Swiss impose yet another responsibility on families. Their code says: "The head of the family is liable for any damage caused by minors unless he can prove that he has given the customary amount of supervision and the care required by the circumstances of the case." This means that parents or others in charge of minors must pay whatever costs are incurred as a result of their minor's misbehaviour, be it graffiti, vandalism, theft, physical abuse, doctor's bills for victims, or the cost of prosecution and jail. This is only right in a just society.

Similarly, the Swiss treat the unemployed in a more responsible way than we do. Workers and employers contribute toward an unemployment insurance scheme which pays its way and provides fourteen months' benefits. After that, the worker is cut off benefits until he or she contributes a goodly amount again. There is no welfare at all because the Swiss expect families to look after their own. Only in cases of disability or extreme hardship are taxpayers asked to get involved.

Canada's expensive system of Unemployment Insurance Commission benefits must be trimmed until it is totally self-financing. In 1993, it ran an $8-billion deficit, which came out of Ottawa's general revenues. The tiny changes announced by the Liberals are thoroughly inadequate. Unemployment insurance must become, once again, an insurance scheme. Workers who routinely dip into its coffers should pay ever-increasing premiums because they are "high risk." The same applies to employers who lay off workers constantly, knowing that they will be subsidized off the job by unemployment insurance. Some Scandinavian countries also do a good job when it comes to unemployment. They require anyone receiving benefits to work for the government in some unpaid capacity, or else attend training of some sort. After twelve to fourteen months, they can receive neither assistance nor welfare. They cannot apply for unemployment help again for two or more years. This builds in an incentive to retrain or look for a job, and makes individuals take more responsibility for their lives than our open-ended, automatic system of entitlements to the jobless.

RESPONSIBILITIES FOR GOVERNMENTS

The responsibilities of governments must also be redefined. Right now, Canada's political structure is a gigantic version of its welfare state: the central government taps taxpayers in wealthy provinces to give open-ended hand-outs to poorer provinces. Called "equalization payments," these were forged simply to let politicians off the hook. Instead of having to debate and decide each case for extra financial aid individually, a mechanism of automatic largesse was fashioned. This eliminated the need to provide good governance by ensuring that the money was well spent, was truly needed, or represented a fair return on the investment.

There is another fallacy behind Canada's automatic subsidies, which Toronto author and town planner Jane Jacobs dealt with in her 1984 book *Cities and the Wealth of Nations*. She debunked the notion that economic wealth can be created by edict or by central planning of any kind. There is an obvious lesson here for Canada, where wealth from dynamic cities such as Toronto, Vancouver, or Calgary is routinely skimmed and squandered in regions like Atlantic Canada and some of the Prairie provinces. The same erroneous theory has been acted on globally. The idea that prosperity can be kick-started in one region with the money from another has led well-meaning governments, the World Bank, and even the United Nations to squander billions on megaprojects in the Third World. The fact is, pouring billions into the boondocks usually results in boondoggles. Look at the black hole of Canadian regional development — Atlantic Canada — where Nova Scotia offers perhaps the country's finest example of governmental irresponsibility — namely, the Sysco steel mill. By 1993, Sysco, known properly as the Sydney Steel Co., had blown a staggering $2 billion worth of federal and provincial tax dollars in two decades. Employment had fallen from 3,000 in the 1970s to 700 currently, and its $279 million in 1992 losses represented an annual cost of nearly $400,000 per job. It was finally sold at the end of 1993.

Such investments have been made on the misguided assumption that wealth can somehow be "conquered" — a throwback to the era when imperial armies acquired wealth by occupying and then plundering colonies. Politicians continue to use phrases such as "industrial strategies," "meeting targets," "resolution purpose," or "long-range planning" as though girding for battle. "Behind that thinking," Jacobs wrote, "lies a conscious or unconscious assumption that economic life can be conquered, mobilized, bullied, as indeed it can be when it is directed toward warfare, but not when it directs itself to development and expansion."

Wealth creation is more analogous to nature, not warfare. Species fill niches to survive. "And the more niches that are filled in a given natural ecology, other things being equal," Jacobs says, "the more efficiently it uses the energy it has at its disposal and the richer it is in life and means of supporting life."

Only cities generated wealth, Jacobs maintained, through import substitution and finding niches. Unfortunately, politicians exploited the wealth generators in most countries by skimming profits from them to hand over to remote regions. She calls these "transactions of decline" and points out that they typified the Roman and British empires, when military might waned or was not an agreeable option. So bribes were handed out until the money dried up and the empires fell apart. This is also what happened to Russia, and may yet happen to Europe and Canada. The European Union hands out huge subsidies, mostly for agricultural purposes. Canada's equalization payments enshrined a similarly unfair and destructive system to redistribute wealth on a massive scale.

Taxpayers in Ontario, Alberta, and British Columbia pay a significantly higher price to be Canadian than do other residents of this country. A report in fall 1993 by Alberta economists Paul Boothe and Bradford Reid of the University of Alberta in Edmonton quantified exactly who paid what, and to whom, in Canada. It was a rare glimpse into the unjust nature of confederation, from a transfer-payments viewpoint, and showed how transfers, grants, equalization, and a host of other programs have made Canadian citizenship distinctly unequal.

The system is unfair twice because the wealthiest regions of the country get no say as to how efficiently their money is spent by the less fortunate provinces. Designed to allow all provinces to provide identical basic government services, Canada's system has created instead seven equalization dependents whose appetites for cash is insatiable.

A report by Paul Boothe measured three types of transfers. First, those made directly to the provinces, including equalization, CAP (Canada Assistance Plan for social assistance, or welfare), and EPF (Established Programs Financing for health and post-secondary education assistance), totalled $21.4 billion in 1991–92. Second, the report took into consideration transfers from the federal government to individuals, on a province-by-province basis. These tallied a whopping $38.4 billion and included Old Age Security, now-extinct family allowances, and unemployment insurance benefits. Last, and least, were transfers directly to businesses, which amounted to $8.9 billion in the form of grants or subsidies to companies or industries, or for specific projects.

The report came up with net figures in the case of a have-not province by subtracting the amounts provincial taxpayers sent to the federal government from the transfers that flowed back to that province. In the case of a wealthy province, the transfers that flowed from Ottawa to the provinces were subtracted from the tax revenues sent by local taxpayers to Ottawa. All figures compared 1991 inflows and outflows. The highlights include:

— Ontario taxpayers contributed $739 more in taxes than they received back in business, provincial, or individual transfers. Albertans contributed $362 more per person, and British Columbians $348 more per person.

— By comparison, the seven have-not provinces obtained huge benefits. Quebeckers got $405 per person; Prince Edward Islanders $2,745 per person; Newfoundlanders $2,638; New Brunswickers $1,828; Saskatchewaners $1,492; Nova Scotians $998 and Manitobans $984. (The biggest increase in the past few years was in Saskatchewan, which went from net receipts of $299 to $1,492 per person, and in Manitoba, which went from $591 to $984.)

— Business transfers. Ontario got $2.5 billion; Quebec $1.8 billion; Saskatchewan $1.4 billion; Alberta $1.2 billion; Manitoba $649 million; B.C. $628 million; New Brunswick $240 million; Nova Scotia $233 million; Newfoundland $181 million; and Prince Edward Island $84 million.

— Unemployment insurance contributions totalled $17.6 billion, or 46 per cent of all transfers to individuals, up from $8.4 billion in 1982. Highest recipients on a per-capita basis were Newfoundland, $1,410 per person per year; Prince Edward Island, $1,193; New Brunswick, $905; Nova Scotia, $696; Quebec, $642; B.C., $537; Ontario, $444; Alberta, $391; Manitoba, $369 and Saskatchewan, $303.

Canada's fiscal burden has been unfair, too open-ended and too favourable to Quebec. In 1993–94, for instance, equalization payments were trimmed for Quebec and axed for other provinces. Manitoba was chopped to $844 million from $1.075 billion; Nova Scotia to $800 million from $1.049 billion; Saskatchewan to $458 million from $683 million;

while Quebec was reduced slightly to $3.633 billion from $3.743 billion.

Apart from its flagrant favouritism, the transfer program has no mechanisms to punish profligate provinces or programs, much less to regulate inefficiencies. Provinces should be forced to match the cost per capita of the most efficient province first before getting any help. As for business grants, these should be spread around more evenly, if they must be handed out at all. The current system is unfair because subsidies to a business in one region give it a competitive advantage over a business in another region. Unemployment insurance is very damaging because it encourages workers who are chronically unemployed in depressed regions to stay there and be supported by those elsewhere who are gainfully employed but struggling themselves to do the subsidizing.

RESPONSIBILITIES OF TAXPAYERS

There is a great deal of cheating going on, and Revenue Canada has been too lenient and slow to end the abuses. An entire industry which advertises openly in newspapers is devoted to offshore exit strategies. Lawyers and accountants in Canada flourish by setting up expensive trust funds in exotic locales to frustrate tax collectors. Not all offshore trusts should be outlawed, but many of them are merely artifices designed to evade taxes.

Revenue Canada should inform all taxpayers in their annual returns that world income must be reported. It should also outline the penalties — from fines to interest payments and jail sentences — for those caught evading taxes. A series of questions should be put squarely on returns to get around the clever manipulations of lawyers regarding offshore investments. Do you have any world income? Please list your foreign bank accounts or any foreign asset you own — whether financial instrument, real estate, time share, artwork, collectibles, or what-have-you. Please estimate their value as of the filing date. Also, please divulge the whereabouts and value of any such assets over which you have control. And also list the assets in trust or another arrangement to which you, or your dependants, are currently beneficiaries. These questions are not presently asked, which means that people can easily hide assets in trusts or with foreign corporations that are aimed at disconnecting ownership from control, for tax purposes.

Another issue is that of wealthy immigrants, mostly from Asia, who live in big houses and use our entitlements. Accountants inform me that they routinely hide their world income, despite huge wealth — which is against Canadian laws. "All Revenue Canada has to do is to ask the immigrants to account for the wealth which they claimed to possess before they immigrated," suggested one accountant. Believe it or not, that is not currently done. The result is excessively high taxation on Canadians who are employed, and too little on well-heeled tax evaders. Revenue Canada should request cooperation from jurisdictions around the world. If denied, Ottawa should stop immigration from those countries until their tax departments share income information. This would stop the practice of people who move their families to Canada, but actually run companies in Hong Kong, Malaysia, or Taiwan without declaring the world income and paying taxes on it.

The government should also crack down on Canadians who live outside the country part of the year. Many snowbirds routinely stay beyond their 181-day limit in Florida, Arizona, Mexico, or wherever. They should be forced to record their border crossings so that their movements can be tracked. They should also have to provide their own medical insurance if they are permanent, part-time residents of another country.

Still others cheat by living more or less permanently just across the border in the United States and use a Canadian address to get medical and other benefits. This practice must be ended and the practitioners found and prosecuted severely.

To increase revenue and stop mass avoidance, Canada should adopt American-style citizenship and tax rules. Canadians can leave permanently, never pay taxes on their offshore income again until they return and, to boot, can come home and enjoy all the benefits and entitlements of Canadian citizenship. This must end. Americans are the only nationality taxed on their worldwide income regardless of where they reside. This means that an American living abroad must pay income tax on his earnings every year. Americans don't pay double taxes because they are credited with whatever tax they paid in the country in which they earned their income.

Of course, Americans can avoid taxes completely by renouncing their citizenship. (Even then the Internal Revenue Services retains the right to make a departed American taxable for up to ten years if it believes the person renounced for tax reasons only.)

Likewise, Canadians should also pay taxes on their offshore income or, alternatively, be allowed to renounce permanently. Then Revenue Canada should set up an élite team to force offshore havens and all other countries to reveal tax returns by Canadian residents to make sure they pay tax here too. That would soon put an end to the K.C. Irving and Bermuda dodge, wealthy Chinese immigrants who leave most of their money offshore, as well as the proliferation of offshore secret bank accounts, trusts, and intermediaries, which protect Canadian tax evaders.

Besides cracking down on tax evasion, Canada must address the fraud and abuse of entitlements such as unemployment insurance, workers' compensation, health care, pensions, and drug benefits. The only effective way to achieve a truly fair, fraud-free, system is to issue a "Canadian residents" card, complete with fingerprint, photo, specimen signature, and a magnetic-strip access to a database. The process for obtaining one of these cards would have to be as rigorous as that regulating the issuance of passports. Only individuals who possessed a card would have access to any of the country's entitlements. The "smart card" would replace the social insurance card, health card, and driver's licence, making it, in the long run, a more efficient method of identification.

A central database would be used to keep track of every individual's use of the system. This would put an end to the double- and triple-dipping by fraudsters, the misuse of drug benefits cards by drug dealers or heavy drug users, as well as the overuse of the medical system.

Some may balk at methods which some describe as reminiscent of "police-state" tactics, but this is the type of security measure that any bank uses. Canadians who balk at such methods simply should not be able to get any entitlements. Without a smart-card system, the country will continue to be ripped off and belief by the public in the country eroded. As things stand now, Canada is not gentler and kinder. It is undisciplined and naïve.

VOLUNTARY UNIONISM AND LABOUR LAW REFORMS

No one should be forced to support financially, much less join, an organization of any kind. The country's Rand Formula must be replaced by legislation that would allow employers, as well as workers, to have the choice of being unionized or not. The country to emulate is the United States which has the best job-creation track record — and lowest unemployment — among all the G-7 nations. Americans create millions of jobs every year by simply deregulating the labour market. This ensures that labour rates are flexible and rise or fall in accordance with supply and demand.

Deregulation recognizes the fact that there is a limit to the wages a country's businesses can afford to pay and that the limit may vary according to market conditions. It also recognizes that wages go up and down in line with the value of the goods and services it produces. Canada's (and Europe's) socioeconomic engineers have fought against these principles, insisting that labour needn't budge in value, and erecting legal impediments to the operation of the market. Europe is so weighted down with regulatory legislation that it stopped creating new jobs years ago.

Canadian union leaders argue incorrectly that deregulation would create a gap between rich and poor similar to that which typifies the United States. That's bunk. Americans spend more on social programs than Canadians do. The gap exists because their sociology is totally different: the United States has a monstrous backward, brutalized underclass of historically disadvantaged minorities. To say America's unique sociological problems, which are an outgrowth of its history, discredit deregulation is a red herring.

The point is, young people, immigrants, or new entrants at low wages don't have to be stuck at the bottom of the heap forever. But continuing with a system in Canada, like Europe's, which is skewed toward artificially high wages has deprived the current generation of job opportunities, and even hope. It has also led to the export of jobs and to some unnecessary automation. All the government has to do is eliminate the following job-robbing policies:

— Impose voluntary unionism. This would give workers the right to pick and choose which union, if any, they wanted to pay dues to. It should also have the effect of destroying the monopoly situation that exists in many sectors at present.

— Reduce entitlements. Canada's excessively generous welfare or unemployment benefits compete against current labour rates because they force wages upward for those who work, with the result that fewer will be employed.

— Legislation must reduce or eliminate the current level of severance, maternity leave, and wrongful/constructive dismissal benefits. For instance, in Ontario, "incompetence" is not grounds for dismissal unless employers have given the worker months of warnings. If they haven't, huge payments (salary in lieu of warnings) must be paid. Under current laws, a two-year employee who hasn't been dogged with paper warnings for months is entitled to three months' wages, which means, once again, that the incompetent cannot be replaced by the company for at least three months because companies cannot pay two people for one job. Even worse, the cost of shedding highly paid "dead wood" results in inaction, so many opt to pay excessive wages to one incompetent who mops up money that could go toward hiring perhaps two or more people.

— Eliminate minimum wages because they destroy jobs for new entrants or unskilled workers. Every increase reduces the number of workers that can be hired out of the money available in the overall corporate cash pool for wages. If a minimum wage is in place, it should fall as unemployment rises.

— Other job-robbers have been the laws that obstruct the right to work without paying union dues, the right to decertify a union if market conditions change, or the right to protect a business from ruin during a strike.

Canada and Europe suffer from a combination of all the ills that would be eradicated by these reforms. Deregulation would lower wages — and prices too. It would reduce inflationary pressure and permit interest rates to fall, thus creating even more jobs.

SUBSIDIARITY

Another impediment to solving the unity crisis has been Ottawa's steadfast refusal to devolve power to the provinces. Had the federal government moved in this direction, they would have satisfied many Quebec nationalists and stolen much of the thunder from the separatists. The federal government could have maintained stricter control over the provinces in some areas but left them alone in most others, emulating the loose, Swiss-style confederation. Instead, Quebec and others have moved into areas the federal government already occupied and won't surrender. The result is a country with two levels of government doing many jobs that only one government need do. This inefficiency has added both to the cost of government and to the cost of doing business.

The debate until now has been whether Quebec should have special powers and privileges. But the real debate should be why doesn't Ottawa hand over as many powers and privileges as possible. The trouble is, politicians rarely, if ever, volunteer to give up power. So they don't.

Consequently, Canada is burdened by too much government. Canada's federal government, for example, gets 41.9 per cent and provinces 35.1 per cent of the total taxes collected in Canada — more than any other second-tier governments in the industrialized world, according to the Canadian Tax Foundation. The rest of the taxes are divided between local governments, who get 8.9 per cent of totals, plus various social security systems, including unemployment insurance and the Canada Pension Plan, which independently collect another 14.2 per cent.

By comparison, the U.S. federal government collects 39 per cent; state governments 18.8 per cent; local governments 12.6 per cent; and social security systems (old age pensions, unemployment or other separate payroll taxes) 29.5 per cent. Australia's central government dominates, with 79.6 per cent of taxes collected (including all social security collections); states, 16.8 per cent; and local governments, 3.5 per cent. France, Belgium, Ireland, Italy, Japan, the Netherlands, and most other industrialized countries have only two levels of government — a unitary federal state and municipalities. The only similar country is Switzerland, a loose confederation, where the federal system collects 29.6 per cent of taxes; provinces or cantons 21.6 per cent; local governments 16 per cent; and social security systems more than the rest, or 32.8 per cent.

Some European nations have successfully juggled the competing demands for centralization and devolution through a concept known as subsidiarity. This concept was the principal reason why Denmark initially voted down the Maastricht

Treaty in 1992, before reversing itself after the big nations voted to pay huge new subsidies to Denmark and others in return for their support. The basic premise of subsidiarity is that Brussels, or in our case, Ottawa, should have power only over areas that local nations (or provinces) themselves simply cannot regulate efficiently or that need to be coordinated by some kind of overarching federal authority. The onus is on the centralizers to prove that they should do the job, and not the local entities.

"The central government should expect to exercise power only where flows of things or people across borders make such power truly necessary," wrote *The Economist* about subsidiarity. "Maastricht emphasizes the principle of subsidiarity which must, as it is intended, minimize interference from Brussels in the status and authority of national legislatures. The local government has much in its favour. It is better informed about what electors want and it is more accountable. But centralisation may sometimes make sense."

If the same principal were applied to Canada, Ottawa could be seriously downsized, and billions of dollars saved. In the 1992–93 taxation year, for instance, some 30 per cent, or $12 billion out of a deficit of $40.5 billion, could have been eliminated without touching social spending or hurting the economy. This could simply be achieved by eliminating the departments of Environment, Forestry, Energy, Mines, Health, Education, Welfare, Fisheries, and Labour, and by selling all crown corporations, plus eliminating other superfluous grants to the Maritimes and various cultural organizations.

Ottawa's jurisdiction should be restricted to foreign policy, monetary control, defence, citizenship, and immigration. It could serve a small role in coordinating provincial environmental, justice, tax collection, or other cross-border policies.

Ottawa does not need to be in the other areas which provinces are now already involved in regulating.

Subsidiarity, however, means that power should not move only downward, but also upward, to bigger, more efficient entities if a compelling case can be made for it. There are at least eight governments too many in Canada — those of New-foundland, Prince Edward Island, Nova Scotia, New Brunswick, Manitoba, Saskatchewan, the Territories, and the Yukon — which should merge with bigger provincial entities. If equalization payments were eliminated, the have-not provinces would be forced to rationalize and become bigger, more efficient entities. The four Maritime provinces should become one province, and the three prairie provinces one, along with the North.

Failing such reforms, Canada remains one of the world's most overgoverned countries, with eight premiers too many, eight legislatures too many, eight lieutenant-governors too many, and eight bureaucracies too many. Consider that, with only 129,756 people, Prince Edward Island has 32 legislative members; Newfoundland, with 568,474 people, has 52; Nova Scotia, with 899,942, 52 legislators; New Brunswick, with 723,900 people, 58 elected politicians. Collectively, all four have a population of 2.3 million and 194 provincial members. By contrast, Ontario, with 10 million people, has 130 in its legislature. (Mind you, Ontario does have dozens of surplus regional governments which should also be abol-ished.) The West is not best: Manitoba has 1 million people and 57 seats; Saskatchewan 988,928 residents and 66 MLAs. Collectively, the two have a population of 2 million and an equally unjustifiable 123 legislators. By contrast, British Columbia, with 3.28 million, has 75 legislators.

Numbers are a problem because every politician has an

expensive support staff, a fancy expense account, and a pension. Cabinet members have more perks, premiers have huge staffs, and lieutenant-governors extravagant budgets, drivers, protocol officers, security staff, travel allowances, and useless monarchical trappings. The goal should be that Canada have only four provincial governments and only one legislator per 44,000 constituents — as is the case in British Columbia — not one per 12,000 as is the case in Atlantic Canada and the Prairies. By putting into practice the principle of subsidiarity, the country could eliminate whole provinces and most of what the federal government does. This would help solve the problem of both the debt and Quebec.

DEMOCRATIC REFORMS

Canada must also bring about a form of direct democracy it now lacks. The use of free votes for parliamentarians, referendums on issues of importance, and even tele-polling for members of Parliament should be harnessed. Canada's judiciary must also be held accountable through a rigorous process of affirmation by elected officials, such as that which exists in the United States for its judges.

In essence, governments must adhere to the twenty-first-century paradigm: only systems or organizations which treat their citizens like customers, not assets to be plundered, will survive. To put it another way: Canada's voters are like shareholders, and Ottawa is the head office. The only politician in Canada who understands this relationship is Alberta's premier Ralph Klein. Klein's government inherited in 1993 the highest per-capita indebtedness of any provincial government. He chose to slash spending and privatize assets in order to balance the budget in four years. The first decision his government made was to lead by example, and his members of the Legislative Assembly became the first politicians in Canada to give up their fancy pension schemes.

Since then, Klein's approach has been thoroughly businesslike. Shortly after becoming premier, he did what any prospective CEO would do: he got a fix on the actual numbers involved and then worked out how to change them for the better. He convened a team of outside experts, headed by a retired business leader and retired civil servant, to do what oil companies call a "workout" or a huge restructuring scheme designed to stem losses and pay down debts. The team studied the province's accounts for forty-five days and found that Alberta's debts were greater than its assets, and its current deficits were unsustainable without bleeding the private sector to death or forcing it to move. "We knew we didn't have a revenue problem. We collect $10.5 billion a year in taxes and that should be enough. We had a spending problem," he said simply.

Klein outlined his team's action plan, promised legislation that would force balanced budgets onto subsequent governments, axed MLAs' fancy pensions and perquisites, went to the people for a mandate, and won a landslide. One year later, in 1994, after a huge controversy generated by unions and unionized newspapers about the "pain" his plan entailed, polls showed Klein with even more support than he had when he won his majority.

Klein took a pessimistic, worst-case-scenario approach to forecasting his budgets. For instance, he counted on absolutely no revenue increases and explained why: "How can you account for big growth in a high-taxation atmosphere? It's just not going to happen. We budget for no increase and, if we get some, that'll be a windfall that we'll apply to paying down the debt." By comparison, the Liberal federal government announced a budget in February 1994 which contained no cushion for higher interest rates and projected thoroughly unrealistic revenue jumps of 17 per cent in personal income taxes and 19 per cent in corporate collections the first year.

The Liberals are prey to that old Canadian myth that massive economic growth will somehow skate the country onside, fiscally speaking. They also chose to postpone any tough action during 1994 in order to try to get Liberals elected in Quebec. Ottawa should bring the provinces to heel by forcing them to seek its permission, and the Bank of Canada's, before they can borrow any funds outside the country in foreign currencies. This will bring their profligacy to a screeching halt, shore up the value of the dollar, and give some relief to interest rates. But, more important, it will force them to live within their means by slashing spending and raising taxes. By postponing such needed actions, the Liberals have condemned Canadian taxpayers to another $65 billion in collective government deficits on top of the $650 billion we already owe.

Klein's approach is the only one that can work. He refuses to procrastinate and treats his electorate like shareholders. He even issues quarterly reports which compare the province's actual financial performance with projections. He explains his philosophy: "When we started as a government we felt we simply had no choice. As the Chinese proverb says: 'Unless we change direction we will likely end up where we are headed.'"

The country will either have a full-blown debt collapse, possibly precipitated by a Quebec entanglement, or experience a gradual decline in living standards through a combination of debts, devaluation, unemployment, and the exodus of talented people and capital.

Fortunately, there are signs that a massive economic correction is already under way. Union and political power is being questioned as never before by Canadians, and also at the ballot box. The flight of money out of the country is sending a serious signal to politicians who choose to listen. And some, such as Ralph Klein, are hearing the message. More important, Canada will be forced to correct its problems because it can never again live in economic isolation. Free trade is now global in addition to continental, and governments, like corporations, are increasingly going to be forced to match the competition, in terms of tax rates and business climate.

I remain optimistic that Canadians will survive no matter what happens, and that this incredibly rich piece of real estate that 27 million of us occupy will continue to yield wealth — but only if we are good stewards and elect leaders who worry about the next generation, not the next election. Failing that, Canadians will face a crisis in this decade which will bring an abrupt end to our national spending binge. It is unfortunate that we will have to learn the hard way what other countries have already learned. It remains ironic that a crisis may save the country. But the root causes of the debt problem must be fixed too. Canada must convert itself from an arrogant, colonial, and paternal system to a fully fledged democracy where individual rights and responsiveness are a permanent countervail to the tyranny of élitist governments. If this doesn't happen, the country is doomed. And deserves to be.